The Last Sharia Court in Europe

The Last Sharia Court in Europe

A Jurist's Travelogue

Maurits Berger

The Hague
2021

Published, sold and distributed by Eleven
P.O. Box 85576
2508 CG The Hague
The Netherlands
Tel.: +31 70 33 070 33
Fax: +31 70 33 070 30
e-mail: sales@elevenpub.nl
www.elevenpub.com

Sold and distributed in USA and Canada
Independent Publishers Group
814 N. Franklin Street
Chicago, IL 60610, USA
Order Placement: +1 800 888 4741
Fax: +1 312 337 5985
orders@ipgbook.com
www.ipgbook.com

Eleven is an imprint of Boom uitgevers Den Haag.

Visual material: *Portrait of a Thracian mufti* and 3D recordings of the courtroom and the surroundings of the sharia court of Komotini can be viewed at www.boomdenhaag.nl/webshop/the-last-sharia-court-in-europe and via the QR code on page 57.

ISBN 978-94-6236-213-0
ISBN 978-90-8974-664-1 (E-book)

© 2021 Maurits Berger | Eleven

This publication is protected by international copyright law. All rights reserved. No part of this publication may be reproduced, stored in a retrieval system, or transmitted in any form or by any means, electronic, mechanical, photocopying, recording or otherwise, without the prior permission of the publisher.

FOREWORD

Ever since I had taken up the two majors of Arabic and Law, I have been fascinated by Islamic law, better known today as 'sharia'. At law school we were also taught Roman and medieval Frankish law, and we got extensive courses in comparative law. In studying all these legal systems, I never felt the need to decide which legal system would be the best. I happened to have grown up in the 20th century in Western Europe, and I do not know any other legal system better than the one applicable there and then, and it suits me just fine. My fascination was with the question of why people all over the world deal with similar relationships – contracts, marriage, tort, property – but have developed such different ways to regulate them.

I studied Islamic law extensively from its medieval Arabic texts and later conducted research into its practice, first in the Middle East, where I lived for seven years and, since 2002, also in the Netherlands and in Europe. The European discussion is dominated mainly by the *sharia councils* in England. They are often referred to as 'sharia courts', which is an incorrect term that often leads to erroneous assumptions, because sharia 'courts' – i.e. courts recognized by the state and authorized to administer justice – do not exist in Europe. At least, that is what I thought. So how surprised was I to learn of the sharia courts in Western Thrace, the eastern province of Greece.

This book is the account of my impressions and experiences of three study trips I made to Western Thrace between February 2018 and June 2019. The story you are about to read is set in this period, whereby I have sometimes taken the liberty of adjusting the chronology of events to fit the storyline. I have also changed the names of some individuals to protect their privacy.

When I studied in the 1980s and 1990s, Islamic law was something exotic and far removed from life in the Netherlands. In that sense it was not unlike Roman or Frankish law. But that was about to change drastically. Sharia has become part of my Dutch society and of most other European societies as well. It has given rise to a host of questions that are still being discussed in politics, courtrooms, the media and in the public domain: Why would people want this so-called sharia? What do they mean by that? Is it permissible?

In Europe, where most inhabitants have become increasingly disconnected from religion and where many regard religion as something backward, these are confusing questions that are often dismissed with terse answers like 'not here!' and 'not again!'. I find these discussions not only interesting, but also very telling of who we Europeans are and who we want to be. To me, therefore, the study of 'Islam in Europe' is not limited to the theological and legal technicalities of that religion and about the struggle for identity by its believers. The debates, responses and interactions by West-European societies with 'Islam in Europe' are an intricate part of that Islam. As an academic I cannot dissociate my research from these debates and responses: together with the desires and actions by Muslims, they create a dynamic that forges an 'Islam in Europe'.

'Islam in Europe', therefore, is not limited to the community of its believers, nor to an exclusive group of specialized scholars. For that reason, I made the deliberate choice to write this book in such a way that it can be read by a wider audience. At the same time, I try to uphold the academic standards of scientific facts and scholarly knowledge and methodology. This endeavour does, however, present me with some academic difficulties, for in order to do justice to all the issues involved in the subject matter, this project should be a multi- and interdisciplinary research, combining law, sociology, political science, history, anthropology and sometimes even psychology. I certainly do not pretend to have mastered all these disciplines, but neither do I want to let that lack of knowledge stop me. I prefer to use a multidisciplinary approach with the risk of stumbling over my ignorance here and there rather than a monodisciplinary approach in which I am sure that all sorts of relevant issues will be left out of the picture. To make this project not only multidisciplinary but also multidimensional, I was accompanied during one of my travels by a film-maker. The *Portrait of a Mufti* and some three-dimensional footage can be seen by the reader using the QR code on page 57.

To do justice to this method, I have opted for a personal approach. It is my conviction that scholars who conduct research on other people can never be strictly objective. One's own background and personal views are bound to play a role, no matter how objective the scholar tries to be. Rather than trying in vain to appear neutral, I believe that, as a scholar, it is better to clarify where I stand, what my surprises are and why, so that the reader can distinguish these personal considerations from factual reporting.

To improve readability, I have used as few footnotes as possible. At the end of the book, however, I do provide literature suggestions for those who wish to delve further into the various topics covered.

Word of thanks
I am very grateful to all the people in Greece, who were so welcoming. My thanks go first to Angeliki Ziaka, associate professor at Aristotle University in Thessaloniki. Our collaboration over the years has grown into a friendship. She introduced me to the world of Thracian Muslims and was so kind to open her extensive network of contacts to me. Selin (not her real name because she preferred to remain anonymous) has been a treasure trove of knowledge and insights, and I gratefully availed myself of her readiness to talk to me any time. Ioannis Androutos, lawyer in Thessaloniki, acted as my liaison with the mufti of Komotini and provided me with ample background information about the sharia court in Komotini. Konstantinos Tsitselikis, professor of international human rights at Macedonia University in Thessaloniki, who, as president of the Greek Human Rights League, advocated changes in the practices of sharia in Greece and, as lawyer, brought the Molla Sali case before the European Court of Human Rights, patiently answered all my questions despite the burden of his own workload. In the Netherlands, Geran Kaay's critical remarks were very helpful, and I am grateful to my publisher who was prepared to embark on the adventure of publishing a book that is academic but, at the same time, not quite so. Above all, however, I am indebted to my brother Pim Berger, to whom I dedicate this book: his inspiration and support made it possible for me to take the first steps in this project and complete it with this book.

CONTENTS

I.	THE COURT CASE	11
II.	THE MUFTI OF KOMOTINI	35
	VIDEO FOOTAGE	57
III.	THE TURKISH DIMENSION	59
IV.	RETURN TO WESTERN THRACE	79
	FURTHER READING IN ACADEMIC LITERATURE	107
	ABOUT THE AUTHOR	117

CHAPTER I

THE COURT CASE

The pen scratches across the paper from right to left. The old man sits hunched over the wooden desk, his eyes behind thick glasses fixed on the movements of the pen, the tip of his tongue between his lips. The silence in the small office is disturbed only by the second man who moves large folders from his desk to the cabinets behind them, where dozens of files are stacked up in disorderly and unsteady piles. There is a palpable tension between the skinny old clerk, who makes himself small behind his desk, and his slightly younger colleague who manoeuvres his corpulent body between the desks and the cabinets and, with broad gestures, arranges the folders.

The old clerk puts down his pen, takes off his glasses and sighs deeply, as if he has been holding his breath too long. With a satisfied look, he reads the text, which is no more than five lines. Then he glances at no one in particular and says: 'It's done. They are divorced, and the man needs to pay the rest of the bridal gift.' No one could check what he was saying because the writing may be recognizable as Arabic script but is in Ottoman, the Turkish language of the Ottoman Empire. This has not been spoken or written anywhere since 1928. Except in the remote town of Komotini, in eastern Greece. It is the language of the only Sharia court in Europe, here, at the south-eastern tip of the European continent.

The old clerk closes the book and puts it aside. 'This was the last ruling of the judge this week. The book can be taken to the Greek court for translation and validation.' The younger clerk picks up the book and opens it. He flips through pages of short texts that are separated by long pencil lines across the page. Those are the court rulings. 'I'll have the judge check it.' The old clerk looks up with a faint smile: surely, he had translated the judge's ruling directly from the Turkish that the judge had spoken in court into the Ottoman that is written down in the book? But he says nothing. Without looking at him, the young clerk squeezes his belly between the two desks and walks out of the room.

The clerks' office leads to a small vestibule that opens up to the entrance from a courtyard. Opposite the clerk's office is the door to the office of the *mufti*, the Islamic judge. The vestibule is crowded with people waiting for their turn to enter the mufti's office. The clerk wriggles past them and enters his office without knocking. That room is larger than the office of the two clerks, about 10 by 6 metres. Windows cover the side bordering the courtyard, with benches underneath. Against the opposite wall is a bookcase. And in between, in front of the back wall, is the large desk of the mufti. Across the entire width of the room is a rug with a dark red Persian motif. For some time now the mufti's office has doubled as the courtroom. The mufti is old, around 80, and he finds the official courtroom, which is on the other side of the courtyard, too cold, especially in the winter months.

There are two people arguing and gesticulating in front of his desk. Four people sitting on the benches under the windows every now and then intervene in their conversation. The mufti listens while leafing through papers on his desk. The clerk walks up to him, bends down and whispers something in his ear while he puts the book on top of the papers the mufti is reading. While the conversation on the other side of the desk continues, the mufti reads the short text in the book, nods and the clerk takes it away.

At the same time in Strasbourg, 1,500 kilometres as the crow flies north-west of this Sharia court in Komotini, a Greek Muslim case is playing out in a completely different court. It is autumn 2017 and the European Court of Human Rights is considering the case of the widow Molla Sali, who lives in the Komotini area. The legal question is simple: does the inheritance of her deceased husband fall under the Islamic or Greek law of inheritance? The Molla Sali couple are Muslims from the Greek region of Western Thrace. According to Greek law, the Islamic family and inheritance law applies to these

Muslims. This law had been applied by one of the three Sharia courts there. However, Mr. Molla Sali had his will drawn up not by the mufti, in accordance with Islamic law, but by a Greek notary, in accordance with Greek law.

According to that Greek will, Molla Sali's widow receives the entire inheritance. If the will had been made according to Islamic law of inheritance, she would have received only one-fourth of the inheritance. Mr. and Mrs. Molla Sali had no children, and when Mr. Molla Sali died, his only heirs were his wife and his two sisters. According to Greek inheritance law, these sisters are excluded from the inheritance. But according to Islamic inheritance law, they would be entitled to three-fourths of the inheritance, and the widow would receive the remaining one-fourth. The differences in outcome between Greek and Islamic law were substantial and prompted the sisters to go to court. They argued that their brother's will was illegal, as it was drawn up according to Greek inheritance law, while the Greek law stipulated that it should have been drawn up in accordance with Islamic law. They pursued their case all the way to the Greek Court of Cassation. The Court of Cassation agreed with the sisters: Greek law stipulates that Islamic family and inheritance law applies to the Muslims in this region of Greece, so this law should have been adhered to. The widow Molla Sali did not leave it at that and is now pleading her case before the European Court of Human Rights. Her argument is that Islamic inheritance law is discriminatory and therefore should not be applicable at all.

The hearing takes place in December 2017 in the Grand Chamber of the futuristic shiny building of the Court in Strasbourg. There is no cacophony of talking witnesses and parties as in the Sharia court in Komotini, nor are there clerks walking into the chamber to interrupt the judge. It is a quiet affair, and the judges listen attentively to the various pleas. The issue is more complicated than it seems at first glance. The lawyer representing the Greek state explains it again. At the beginning of the 20th century, Greece and Turkey signed a series of treaties establishing the rights of their mutual minorities: the rights of the Turkish-Muslim minority in the eastern tip of Greece, and the rights of Greek Orthodox in the western tip of Turkey, particularly in Istanbul. In the case of Greece, this means that the

Muslims who have lived there for generations may retain their own language (Turkish) and religion (Islam), including the teaching thereof and the administration of justice. This Islamic jurisdiction only concerns family and inheritance law, and for this purpose the Greek state recognizes three 'sharia' courts and appoints Islamic leaders – muftis – as judges.

This situation has existed for almost a century, says the lawyer emphatically, and to deviate from it means that Greece would be in breach of its international obligations. And Greece prefers not to have any unnecessary quarrels with a treaty partner like Turkey, with whom relations are already so sensitive. This last observation is not made by the lawyers in so many words, but it is clear to everyone. The judges are going to deliberate. The verdict is expected in a year's time.

In the meantime, a huge debate has erupted on this issue in Greece, but also in the rest of Europe. The Molla Sali case is making headlines everywhere. Suddenly, the spotlight of Europe is on that small Greek region called Thrace, located in the very east of Greece. This tip of Europe, known since Greek mythology as 'Thrace', is divided into an eastern part, which is in Turkey (where Istanbul is located), a northern part, in Bulgaria, and a western part, in Greece. That is why the Greek part is also referred to as 'Western Thrace' which can be confusing as it lies in the most eastern part of Greece. It is a narrow strip of land, 150 kilometres long and 30 to 50 kilometres wide. It is bordered to the south by the Aegean Sea, to the north by a mountain range that forms the border with Bulgaria and to the east by Turkey. Seen from the Greek angle, this region resembles a dead-end corridor. And that is how it has been treated for a long time.

The discussions in Europe concern the existence of courts applying Islamic family law in a modern European country. The situation in Western Thrace had long been known to some scholars and human rights lawyers. But most Greeks were hardly aware of it, and the rest of Europe even less so. But now everyone is shocked: Huh? Sharia on the European continent?! And we are not talking about something that has recently been imported from abroad, as is the case with so-called 'sharia councils' in the United Kingdom. No, this has been around for a long time in the backyard of the European continent. What is more, it is a recognized part of the Greek legal system.

For more than thirty years I have been researching Islamic law, or sharia as it is also known – first in the Middle East, where I studied it for intermittent periods at the Law Faculty of Cairo University, the Sharia Faculty of Damascus University and in a mosque in the inner city of Damascus. When I moved back to the Netherlands in 2002, I shifted my research to sharia in Europe. It is a subject that is highly sensitive. Many people seem to think that sharia is something of the Taliban and Saudi Arabia, and since early 2000 there has been great concern that such practices would also be introduced into Europe by Muslim migrants. There were reports about so-called *sharia councils* in England, but the commotion on this subject was sparked in 2004, with the news of the intention to establish a *sharia tribunal* in the Canadian state of Ontario. In the Netherlands this led to anxious questions in the Dutch parliament, and the government commissioned an investigation into the possible existence of sharia jurisprudence in the Netherlands. The report, which came out in 2010, concluded that there was no such thing. Imams were regularly called in to resolve marriage disputes, the report concluded, but not in an institutionalized fashion by means of courts or councils or the like. This proved also to be the case in in other West-European countries.

The situation was quite different in the United Kingdom. The British government had shown great concern with the emergence of the sharia councils, that is, organizations of Muslim scholars who offer their legal advice and services to Muslims who might be in need of them. The British government commissioned various studies into this phenomenon. The outcomes were not conclusive. Strictly speaking, Muslims were free to make use of the services provided by these sharia councils. Women, in particular, made use of them, because, unlike men, they had no means under Islam to end a marriage by themselves. But the studies were highly critical of the discriminatory rules of Islam these women were subjected to by the councils, the conservative and condescending conduct of the 'judges' of these councils towards the women, and the pressure from the community towards these women to submit their case to a sharia council rather than to a British court.

The apprehension about sharia in Western Europe was directly linked to security concerns that followed the attacks of 11 September 2001 in America. The notion of sharia was considered to be part of Muslim radicalism. That was the reason that alarm bells went off among terrorism experts in 2003 when it turned out that quite a few young Muslims in Western European countries entered into so-called 'Islamic marriages' without registering them at the civil registry. According to the terrorism experts, it was common for a young Muslim man preparing for a suicide attack to contract an Islamic marriage so that he could say goodbye to a full life. Politicians were also concerned, but for different reasons: they wondered whether the Muslims' non-registration of their marriage constituted a rejection of European society. In my country, the Netherlands, the government yet again commissioned a report on the matter. The study appeared in 2009 and showed that the non-registration was not meant to prepare for a suicide mission or to reject society but was the result of young Muslims finding alternative ways to arrange relationships. Couples that wanted to have a sexual relationship or cohabit without taking the big step of a full marriage opted for an Islamic marriage without registration. Later studies showed that Islamic marriage sometimes also served other purposes, such as thwarting the plans of parents to hook their daughter up with an undesirable marriage partner. Rules of Islam played a role for the pious, but apparently also for the devious.

In Greece, however, something else seemed to be at play than in the United Kingdom or the Netherlands, or any other European country. Here, Islamic family law was not practised in parallel with the existing national law but was a recognized part of the Greek legal system. That was unlike anywhere in Europe. All the more reason for me to pack my bags and take a closer look.

One of the lawyers who had brought the case of the widow Molla Sali before the European Court of Human Rights lives in Thessaloniki, a large, lively city that serves as the centre of northern Greece. From here, a new motorway leads eastwards to the region of Western Thrace, where the Greek Muslims live. The inhabitants of Western Thrace have long depended on Thessaloniki for the university, the hospital and the airport. Since the 1970s there is also a university in Komotini and an airport in the town of Kavala. But Thessaloniki remains the 'big city' of this northern region of Greece.

Thessaloniki, also known as Saloniki, was known for centuries as one of the great 'Jewish' cities in Europe. Most Jews had migrated here from Europe to escape persecution and discrimination. A great wave of Jews arrived from Spain after they were banished from there in 1492. They were welcomed with open arms by the Ottomans, who thought the Spaniards were crazy to expel a community in possession of such rich trading houses and networks throughout Europe and the Middle East. The Ottomans resettled these Jews in cities such as Thessaloniki and would indeed gain a great economic advantage by doing so. Later, in the 18th and 19th centuries, this Jewish community was augmented by the Jews who fled the pogroms in Russia. During the Second World War, however, the Nazis deported the entire Jewish population of Thessaloniki to death camps.

Since then, little remains of the city's Jewish character, or its Ottoman legacy, for that matter. Greek Orthodox churches now dominate the streets, as do the many shops and cafés. The city's atmosphere is noticeably coloured by the students of the two universities. On the way from the bus stop to my hotel in Thessaloniki, I am surprised to see two young people walking in the street with Arab lutes. They are not bouzoukis, but real Arab lutes, as I know them from the Middle East. Curious, I stop them and inquire about their instruments. They are Greek conservatory students, and tonight they are giving a performance to mark the end of the academic year. You are very welcome, they say, and admission is free.

But, first, I have an appointment with the lawyer, Konstantinos Tsitselikis. When I contacted him by email, he pointed out that he is not a practising lawyer, but a professor of international human rights at one of the two universities in Thessaloniki. He is quite the human rights activist and has spent much time reconciling the practice of sharia in Greece with human rights. The Molla Sali case was a spin-off of those efforts and an exceptional episode in his academic career.

He lives with his family in a small flat in an apartment block. Several bookcases in the corner of the large sitting room separate the family's living space from his small office. The chaos of books and papers is surprising for a lawyer who has just successfully guided his client through the first phase of the complex legal process before the European Court of Human Rights. He sees the look on my face and says with a crooked smile: 'This mess is typical for any university professor, isn't it?' He offers me his desk chair and sits on a stool after removing the pile of papers on it.

His wife is out for work and he has a daddy's day. His son is having fun with Lego, but his little daughter is begging for attention. Fortunately, the chocolate I brought works wonders: she happily retreats to a corner, where she sits and starts to nibble. For the next hour we can talk without interruption. Konstantinos thinks it is a shame that a modern state like Greece allows a legal system that discriminates between men and women. By this he means the Islamic family law that applies in Western Thrace. He is also concerned about the procedural side of the proceedings in the sharia courts: 'Apparently, these judges can just go ahead and make their own decisions, without any rules of procedure or possibilities of redress.'

Something else that bothers Konstantinos is that Muslims in Western Thrace do not seem to have the possibility to choose. 'If we have this darned Islamic family law in Greece, can a Muslim at least have the right *not* to have it applied?' That was also the main argument in his defence of the widow Molla Sali. Unlike the Greek Court of Cassation, Konstantinos was of the opinion that Islamic family law is not compulsory for Muslims in Western Thrace.

But at the moment of my visit this argument had already become obsolete: the Greek parliament had passed a law in January 2018, shortly after Molla Sali's hearing in Strasbourg, giving Muslims in Western Thrace the right to choose between Islamic and Greek civil law. Case closed, one might say. This had happened several weeks before my arrival in Thessaloniki. Konstantinos was indeed satisfied with this unexpected turn of events, and even a little proud: it was quite something for a human rights activist like him to get parliament to change a law before the court case has even been concluded. But this meant that Islamic law still existed in Greece. For Konstantinos, the next step was to do something about that: 'Some colleagues think it should be abolished. I don't think so, as long as it is brought in line with the principles of human rights.'

On my way back to the hotel my taxi gets stuck in a traffic jam. The driver tries to circumvent it by taking backstreets, but the entire city centre seems cut off. In the distance we hear a swelling noise of shouting crowds and the whinnying of horses. The taxi driver grins and shrugs his shoulders and explains in halting English that the Greek government has just reached an agreement with its neighbour, the Former Yugoslav Republic of Macedonia, that it will change its name to North Macedonia. There is a lot of opposition here in Greece because people think that the name Macedonia belongs to the Greek. 'Thessaloniki is the capital of the province of Macedonia, and this region is part of our Greek history. After all, it is the birthplace of Alexander the Great.'

Several blocks away we see the demonstrating crowd crossing the street. Men on horseback are waving Greek flags and flags of the Greek province of Macedonia. 'Those guys have come all the way from Crete.' It is clear that the resentment against this decision is deeply felt. And all this because neighbouring Macedonia wants to keep its name? I must have sounded a bit sceptical, because the driver says sternly: 'That country is not called Macedonia, but the former Yugoslav Republic of Macedonia. That is their official name. Macedonia, that's us.' His face shows no trace of humour.

That same evening, I take a rickety lift to a cramped room on the top floor of a rundown apartment building. It is the place pointed out to me by the young musicians. About eighty young people have gathered there, sitting on the floor and on folding chairs. The atmosphere is friendly and hippie-like and reminds me of my stay-overs as a kid with my uncle, who was a student in the 1970s. A fragile-looking female singer is flanked by young musicians who play Arabian lute, violin, bouzouki and hand drum. The nasal singing and the music give me a jolt of nostalgia: this is what I know from Syria, where I had lived for four years. But no, I am assured, this is perfectly Greek. It is old music from the eastern islands and also from the Greeks who were forced to migrate from Turkey in 1923. This folk music is becoming more and more popular among the young, I am told.

From Thessaloniki to Kavala is an hour and a half's drive on a newly constructed highway. Kavala is the last town one passes through before entering Thrace. It is a pretty coastal town with some tourism. It is also the port for the ferry to the island of Thassos, which lies just off the coast and during summers is swamped by tourists from Romania, Bulgaria and Serbia. The large roundabout in the centre of town is dominated by a 50-metre-high brick aqueduct that towers over the traffic. Underneath the aqueduct, in the middle of the roundabout stands a huge sign with the inscription 'Constantinople, 460 km' and an arrow pointing eastwards. Constantinople? That was the ancient name of the capital of the Byzantine Empire, until the city was conquered by the Ottomans in 1453 and renamed Istanbul. More than five centuries later the Greeks apparently still cling to the ancient name of the city that was the epicentre of Greek Orthodox Christianity for centuries.

Nevertheless, Ottoman history is omnipresent in Kavala. The Ottomans ruled this region for more than 500 years. The aqueduct may be described as Byzantine by the locals, but it probably dates from Roman times, fell into disuse under the Byzantines and was restored and put to use again by the Ottomans in the 16th century. The fortress that rises above the town is also Ottoman and dates from those times. So is the *imaret*, the huge complex that housed both schools and *hammams*. It is now a luxurious hotel where guests feel as if they are living in a thousand-and-one-night world.

While the Greeks know Kavala as the last stop before entering Thrace, and Kavala for the tourists is the transit port to tourist destinations, it is known to the Egyptians as the birthplace of the founder of modern Egypt: Mohamed Ali. He was an officer in the

Ottoman army and was stationed in Kavala until 1801, when he was sent with an expeditionary army to the Ottoman province of Egypt to drive out Napoleon, who had just invaded the country with his army. However, by the time Mohamed Ali landed in Egypt, Napoleon had already withdrawn. Mohamed Ali made use of the confused state of affairs to establish himself as the new ruler in Cairo. He started an ambitious project of modernization and founded a dynasty of rulers that would last until 1952. Egyptians still regard him as the founder of modern Egypt.

In a small church in Kavala, a child is baptised. The church is packed with family and friends wearing their best clothes. Baptism is an important event in the Greek Orthodox community. The special thing here is that the child is seven years old. That is a bit old to be baptised. But he and his family live in America, and they had never come around it. According to some, his Greek mother is not very religious, but once she decided that he needed to be baptised she was adamant that it should take place in her hometown of Kavala. According to others, it was her very religious family that had insisted on this.

The boy stands shivering in a large brass baptismal font which has been placed on the ground for the occasion. He is wearing only swimming trunks and has his eyes lowered in shame. He shudders when the priest scoops a bowl of water from the font and pours it over him. The crowd cheers and claps. The boy is quickly wrapped in a towel, while the aunts rush to kiss him. The gathering then heads outside to the cars that will take them to the restaurant, where a roasted goat awaits them.

The American father endured everything with a smile. He is used to going along with the traditions that are so dear to the Greeks, especially those who have emigrated, like his wife. She had gone to study in America, like so many Greeks, and stayed there. But when they wanted to get married, it had to be in Greece, in the place where the bride was born, in the presence of the whole family. There was only the question of his religion, for he was a Methodist. Of course, they could also have had a civil marriage because since 1982 Greeks can choose between a civil and a religious marriage, both of which can be registered as valid marriages (that was a surprise to me, coming from a legal system inherited from Napoleon, where only civil marriages can be registered). But the Greek family insisted on a religious marriage. That meant, however, that the American groom had to become Greek Orthodox, because Greek Orthodox religious law does not allow mixed marriages.

The ban on mixed religious marriage is typical for almost every religious law. The reason is simple: many religions want to keep their community of believers intact and therefore forbid them to marry outside that community. If you, as a believer, want to marry someone who has a different religion, then that marriage partner must convert to your religion. Catholics require both spouses to be Catholic, Orthodox requires both partners to be Orthodox. Islam only requires the non-Muslim man to convert to Islam if he wants to marry a Muslim woman; Jewish or Christian women who marry a Muslim man do not need to convert to Islam but can maintain their own religion.[1] The problem, of course, is that these requirements work both ways. The religion of the other marriage partner may very well have similar demands about both spouses belonging to that one religion. As a consequence, one of the partners will have to give in and convert to the religion of the other partner in order for their marriage to be religiously valid. An extra complication, then, is that such conversion will be considered an act of apostasy by the religion that is being abandoned. These are just a few of the complexities of mixed religious marriages.

In the 1950s this situation led to a special situation in the Egyptian city of Alexandria. This city had a community of tens of thousands of Greeks and Italians who had lived there for generations. The Greeks

---

[1] The reason for this different treatment of men and women has to do with Islam's views on the transmission of religion. According to Islam, the children follow the religion of the father. Consequently, the children of a Muslim man will be Muslim (and their mother's religion has no role in this), whereas the children of a non-Muslim man would have his religion (hence the requirement for him to convert to Islam in order for his children to be Muslim).

were Orthodox, the Italians Catholic. Although both communities were substantive in numbers, each had too few marriage partners to suit the need in their own group. Since marrying a Muslim was out of the question for them, the next best option was to marry a Christian of a different sect. As a result, there were many mixed Greek-Italian marriages which were effectively Orthodox-Catholic marriages. These were concluded in accordance with either Catholic or Orthodox law (civil marriage did not exist), and people did not bother with the strict rules of conversion: they were all Christians, and that was what mattered.

But this backfired in 1952, when such a Orthodox-Catholic couple wanted to divorce. Divorce would normally not be an option for either of them, because both Catholic and Orthodox law do not allow divorce. But a clever lawyer found a solution to this problem: did not both legal systems stipulate that a mixed religious marriage was forbidden? Orthodox law does not allow a marriage with a non-Orthodox, and Catholic law does not allow a marriage with a non-Catholic. But that was what had happened in this marriage because both spouses had kept their own religion. Then this marriage should never have been concluded in the first place! The couple's marriage was nullified by both the Catholic and the Orthodox family courts, but this set in motion a flood of nullity applications by Catholic-Orthodox couples who finally saw a possibility for divorce. This led to such unrest within the Italian and Greek communities of Alexandria that the Islamic family court felt the need to step in. The Islamic court was normally only for Muslims (the Orthodox and Catholics had their own courts in Egypt) but in this case acted as the national court that was to uphold public order. The Islamic court considered that the Catholic and Orthodox communities in Egypt were entitled to have their religious family laws, to be applied by religious courts, and that the annulments issued by these Catholic and Orthodox family courts were therefore legally valid. But, the Islamic court held, the application of these laws should not lead to the disruption of the community. The court therefore banned the practice of these annulments.

Alexandria was an unusual case, but it illustrates how a mixed religious marriage can create all sorts of legal, family and theological problems. The simplest solution was, therefore, conversion by one of the partners, so that both partners had the same religion. Often, the one who has least affinity with religion will conform to this solution. In the case of the Greek marriage in Kavala, it was the American husband who gave in. He did not care much for his own Methodist background and agreed to convert to the Greek Orthodox religion. Prior to their marriage, therefore, the festive ceremony of his conversion had to take place. His American family attended the rituals and the subsequent festivities, bewildered by the Greek religious practices and traditions that seemed utterly alien to them.

I leave Kavala and continue eastwards along the highway that cuts the length of Thrace. But it is not clear to me where West Thrace begins. There are no signs along the road. On a few hills and mountain tops I see an occasional lonely cross, sometimes 20 metres high (perhaps to mark that I am still in Christian territory?)

But then I see minarets rising like pencils between the white houses of the villages in the mountain foothills along the road. I leave the motorway and take the smaller roads that connect the villages. One imagines oneself in the Turkish countryside. The older women wear headscarves, and Turkish is spoken everywhere. Only the road signs are in Greek and there are occasional Greek flags on houses and buildings. This is the area where the Greek Muslims live. Greek Orthodox also live there, let us not forget them. But where these Christians regularly go to other parts of Greece for holidays, work, study or family visits, the Thracian Muslims hardly ever go to the rest of Greece. For study they go mainly to Turkey, and for work many young men go to Germany.

Western Thrace has three towns with sharia courts: Xanthi, Komotini and Didymoteicho. The motorway strings these towns together. My destination is the second city, Komotini, but just before Xanthi I stop in a village at a restaurant where I had been ten years earlier with some students. At the time, my university department was participating in a project with other universities where students came together for two weeks to discuss issues of Islam in Europe.

That year, the conference took place in Thessaloniki, and five students had signed up for it. I had teaching obligations in the Netherlands, so I attended only the last four days, together with a colleague. On arrival, I was immediately taken aside by three of my students who were Muslim and wore headscarves: 'It's terrible here, Sir, everyone is so unfriendly.' The latter was quickly confirmed when we walked down the street. An orthodox priest in a black habit and a long beard scolded us as soon as he noticed us. We did not understand his Greek, but his repetition of the word 'Taliban' and his aggressive arm gestures spoke volumes.

I thought it sensible to get away for a day, and I announced that we were going to make a road trip to Western Thrace. We set ourselves two goals: we wanted to visit a sharia court, and the Muslim students wanted to have a halal meal (which they had been unable to find in Thessaloniki). Neither of these goals was achieved. The sharia court was closed, and none of the Thracian Muslims we talked to on the way seemed to understand what we meant by halal. As one of the students was Turkish and acted as our interpreter, there was no problem with communication. After the umpteenth conversation with some villagers, she turned to us with a sad expression: 'They don't have halal meat here either! They just eat meat like everyone else.' The three Muslims looked glum, but the other two students burst out laughing: 'You Dutch Muslims are much more Islamic than the Muslims who have lived here for centuries!'

At lunch that day our company almost caused a diplomatic incident. We were sitting at one of two long tables on the narrow terrace of a restaurant. At the far end of the other table sat a group of young men who kept staring at us. Then one of them stood up and called to us: 'Where you from?' 'Holland!' we answered in unison. The Greeks looked suspicious. They pointed at us one by one and asked each of us: 'Where you from?' Their confusion was understandable, because there were two blond students, three students with headscarves, one of whom was from Turkey, one from Morocco and one from Tunisia, and of the two teachers I was from the Netherlands and the other from Egypt. But with each pointing finger and questioning look of the Greeks we answered with a grinning 'From Holland!' The Greeks, astonished, fell back on their chairs and began to talk among each other in hushed tones, while we continued to eat. Half an hour later the waiter came with a tray of glasses and a bottle of ouzo: 'From the gentlemen at the other table.' The Greeks raised their glasses invitingly. The Muslims at our table whispered in panic: 'We can't refuse, that would be rude. But we don't drink that. Mr Berger, you must drink on our behalf!' But although I do like a glass of beer or wine, I just happen to detest ouzo. The Greeks kept raising their glasses to us. The Muslims at our table panicked: 'We cannot be rude, please do something!' In the end, we furtively poured water into our glasses and raised them to our Greek friends.

The restaurant is still there, unchanged. I sit at one of the two tables outside and place my order. Then I pull out the book that Konstantinos recommended and start reading. It is one of the standard English language works on minorities in Greece. It quickly became clear that to understand the current situation, we have to go back in time. Way back.

Already in antiquity the Greeks were a diaspora people who lived scattered along the coasts of the Mediterranean and the Black Sea and founded settlements or moved to other coastal villages and towns. What united them was their language and culture. In the following centuries, Greek became the lingua franca of the Mediterranean region: it was the language of culture and diplomacy and was spoken in Roman schools, at the Byzantine court, at the Norman court of Sicily and, for a short time, even at the Islamic court of Damascus.

From the 14th century onwards, the Ottoman Empire conquered a large part of the Black and Mediterranean coastal areas, and the Greeks became one of the many peoples living in that empire. The Ottomans did not have the concept of citizenship as the Romans had a millennium earlier. The Ottomans used the *millet system*, in which subjects were divided into religious communities – *millets* – that had autonomy in religious affairs. Each community had its own religious law, often with their own courts. Their leaders were accountable to the sultan. In the European part of the Ottoman Empire – the present Balkans – the Orthodox Christians made up the majority of the population, outnumbering other Christian sects, Jews and even Muslims.

In the 19th century, all these peoples and communities were captivated by nationalism: each considered themselves a single people ('nation') who should have its own territory, its own language and its own flag – but also its own religion. This was one of the reasons why the Serbs, Bulgarians, Greeks and Russians founded their own Orthodox Churches, causing national divisions in the Orthodox Church. But religion and people did not always overlap. Take the Greeks, for instance. What they had in common was the Greek language and the Greek culture that came with it, but while most were indeed Orthodox, some were also Muslim (for instance, on the islands of Kos and Rhodes) or Jewish (as in Saloniki). The other peoples in the region were confronted with the same situation. These hybrid forms of communities had been common for centuries but were no longer accepted in the 19th century. The result was a series of wars among these nations leading to gruesome forms of ethnic and religious cleansing. From the smoking ruins rose the countries that make up the Balkan states as they are known today.

However, this did not solve the original questions of national identity. Religion and people did not always coincide, but neither did country and people. Greece, for instance, declared its independence in 1821, but many Greeks lived outside its newly established national borders, on the coasts of the Black Sea and in cities like Smyrna in Turkey and Alexandria in Egypt. Something similar was the case with the people known as Turks: the Ottoman Empire shrank during the 19th century to become today's Turkey, which proclaimed itself a republic in 1923, but not all Turks lived in Turkey. Many of them still lived in the Balkans, the Levant and Egypt. Some of them left for what was called the 'homeland', but many remained in the countries that had been their home for generations.

In the case of Turkey and Greece this situation escalated with their war from 1919 to 1922. In each country this war fuelled the mistrust towards the countrymen that were suspected of allegiance to the enemy: the 'Greeks' in Turkey and the 'Turks' in Greece. As part of the peace agreement, in 1923, the two countries therefore decided on a rigorous solution: the exchange of each other's compatriots.

An estimated 1.5 million Greeks were forced to move from Turkey to Greece and half a million Turkish Muslims from Greece to Turkey. Most of them had to leave a country where they had lived for generations, sometimes even centuries. Today, almost a hundred years later, we may look back at this exchange in horror, but at the time it was celebrated as a diplomatic victory: better this than another terrible war, right?

Only a small community of Turks in the Greek province of West Thrace and a small community of Greeks in the Turkish province of East Thrace were exempted from this population exchange. For them, the Treaty of Lausanne (1923) stipulated that these minorities could keep their rights.[2] This included the right to education in their own language and the application of their own religious family law by their own courts. For the Muslims in Greece, this jurisdiction had previously been granted to the muftis.[3] *Muftis* is the term for Islamic scholars who interpret Islamic law. In the case of the Thracian Muslims, however, they also acted as religious leaders and judges. And the judgments they made as Islamic judges on marriage, divorce, custody and inheritance were recognized by the Greek state on an equal footing with the judgments by Greek judges.[4]

This special status is still in place today but applies only to the approximately one hundred thousand Muslims in Western Thrace. No such status was created for Muslims in other parts of Greece, such as the four thousand Greek Muslims living on the islands of Kos and Rhodes. For example, the Muslim community of Kos and Rhodes has its own imams, but no Islamic judges or schools, as is the case

---

2   These rights had already been laid down in the Treaties of Athens (1913) and Sèvres (1920). The Treaty of Lausanne (1923) explicitly dealt with the situation after the exchange of the two populations.

3   Treaty of Athens (1913), Art. 11: 'The muftis, in addition to their authority over purely religious affairs and their supervision of the administration of *vakouf* property, shall exercise jurisdiction between Mussulmans in matters of marriage, divorce, alimony (*néfaca*), guardianship, trusteeship, emancipation of minors, wills of Ottomans, and succession to the office of Mutevelli (*tevliet*). The judgments rendered by the muftis shall be executed by the proper Greek authorities.'

4   Art. 5 of the Greek Law 1920/1991.

with the Muslim minority in Western Thrace. For this reason, Greek official terminology distinguishes between 'Muslim *minority*' for the Muslims in Western-Thrace and 'Muslim *community*' for Muslims on Kos and Rhodes.

To complicate matters further, these two Muslim groups are collectively referred to as 'Old Muslims', as opposed to the 'New Muslims', who are the Muslims who have come to Greece as immigrants in recent decades and who have settled mainly in Athens. These New Muslims, estimated to number two hundred thousand, are more numerous than the Old Muslims. There is no separate regulation for them, but neither is it clear what their status is. One would think that the 'normal' rules of freedom of religion would apply to them, but they are not allowed, for example, to build mosques or maintain an Islamic cemetery. For that, they are referred to Western Thrace.

And even in this complex story the picture is not complete. The Western Thracian Muslims consist of several ethnic language groups, the most numerous being Turks, Pomaks (an ethnic group that also lives in Bulgaria) and Roma. I found it all rather confusing. As a Dutchman, I thought I was used to a complex composition of populations, given our own century-old religious fragmentation with Catholics, various Protestant denominations and Jews, recently extended with Hindus and Muslims, combined with the ethnic diversity with people like the Limburgers and Groningers, and compiled with the linguistic variety of Frisian as a separate language and dozens of dialects. But this here in Western Thrace seems a lot more complicated. Would I remember it all if I started talking to the people involved? I secretly hoped that it would not be relevant any more in modern Greece, but I turned out to be gravely mistaken.

In Xanthi, I have an appointment with Rahmi Basia, head of the imams in the province of Thrace and teacher of Islam at a secondary school. The Mufti of Xanthi is his superior as he is the one who appoints the imams, but Rahmi coordinates the imams' activities. He is in his thirties and very blond – because he is a Pomak, he explains ('and I am proud of it!'). The appointment was made for us by my colleague Angeliki Ziaka, an associate professor at the Aristotle University of Thessaloniki. Ten years ago, when my students had come over for the conference at this university, she had suggested some interesting points to visit during our road trip. It turned out that she was one of the few people in Greece who are knowledgeable about the Thracian Muslim minority and she knows many of them personally. 'That's because of my father,' she had told me. 'He was a professor of comparative religion and he always said that he didn't have to travel far for that comparison because he found it all in his backyard.' As a girl, she had often accompanied him and so had come to know a large number of people in the region.

Since 2013, Angeliki Ziaka had been developing a religious education programme for Western Thrace on behalf of her university department. This, too, had to do with the special status of the Muslim minority there. According to the Treaty of Lausanne, they were entitled to education in their own language and religion.
As a consequence, there were schools with primary and secondary education in Turkish and Greek. Other Muslim minorities in Western Thrace, such as the Pomaks and Roma, also have their own language, but since these are only spoken and not written they attend Turkish-speaking schools. The Greek government had grown increasingly concerned about the lack of integration of the Turkish-speaking Muslim minority in Greek society. But they feel there was nothing they could do because in their view the situation was set in stone by the treaty with Turkey.

A few years ago, however, the government saw an opening. It turned out that more and more children from the Muslim minority were attending Greek public schools. There they were taught in Greek, and this gave them access to higher secondary education in Greece. This was a shift in their traditional look eastwards to Turkey, where they commonly pursued their higher education. Now they were also looking to the west, to the universities of Thessaloniki and beyond, even as far as Athens. This was a development that the Greek government wanted to encourage. To this end, it was going to remove as many obstacles as possible to Muslims attending 'Greek' public schools.

One of these obstacles was the religious education in these public schools. Although these lessons were meant to discuss religion in general, they were still taught mainly from the Christian perspective. In 2013, a new education law was promulgated for the public schools of Western Thrace: Islam was introduced as a separate module in the religion lesson in primary and secondary Greek public schools. However, the religion teachers at these schools were Orthodox and had very limited knowledge of Islam, so they had to receive extra training. At the same time, imams and Islam teachers from Islamic schools were offered positions as religion teachers at Greek public schools. But to qualify, they had to learn the pedagogical tools of how to teach religion, in general, and Christianity and Islam, in particular.

This was the project Angeliki Ziaka was charged with. First, she had to convince Islamic teachers to make the step to the public school. For this she had to nudge them into overcoming their mistrust of the world of the Greeks and Orthodox Christianity, which was utterly new to them. Rahmi Basha was one of the first who had dared to take the step. However, not only Muslim but also Christian teachers were reluctant to learn about another religion, because in this new training programme, *all* religious teachers had to participate, including those from the Greek schools. For the first time, Muslims and Christians were sitting together in a training programme in which they not only learned about each other's religion but were also taught the difference between teaching *into* religion (how it should be according to a particular religion) and teaching *about* religion (what is religion).

At times the joint classes could be confrontational for both sides. Rahmi tells me about the one time during the training that the Christian participants wanted their Muslim colleagues to distance themselves from the violence committed against the Greek Orthodox Church during Ottoman rule. After an interval of silence, a female Muslim teacher said that according to this logic, the Christians should also distance themselves from the misdeeds they had committed against the Muslims. 'What misdeeds?' was the indignant reaction of the Christian teachers. The Muslim teacher mentioned the Crusades and some other examples, and silence fell again. Neither side really knew much about what their forefathers had done to each other in the past. Both sides saw themselves as victims of the other.

At the time I meet Rahmi, the programme has caught on. Following Rahmi's example, more imams and teachers of Islam from the Islamic schools have been trained as teachers of religion in public schools. 'It has succeeded beyond expectation,' Angeliki Ziaka had told me a year earlier. 'That is because those religion teachers are in training together. It serves as a safety valve. That way, latent tensions within as well as between the two communities can be vented.'

Shortly before arriving in Komotini, I make one more stop. Between Xanthi and Komotini is a village where I had arranged to meet Aysel, one of the few female Islamic scholars in Western Thrace. Rahmi had advised me to speak to her and had arranged the meeting during our conversation. He spoke into his mobile phone in Turkish, and when he hung up, he simply said: 'This afternoon, at five. She's teaching then, but you can walk in. Here is the address.' It is the same experience I knew so well from the Middle East, where appointments are never made for the following week but for the same day.

Aysel had completed the imam training in Turkey. This education is different from what Western European countries mean by imam training. In Turkey, it is a long-term education at the university level of people who have already received intensive religious instruction during their secondary schooling. Aysel had followed the Turkish training all the way through to the university graduation but has not become an imam in a mosque. She smiled politely when I asked about it and did not answer. The reason is probably that women are generally not allowed to hold such positions.

Aysel works outside the mosques, in particular by giving catechism lessons. She has arranged for our appointment to coincide with one of these lessons, and when I knock on the door of an outbuilding of a whitewashed neighbourhood mosque at the appointed time, I hear the murmur of voices behind the door. When Aysel opens the door, I see about twenty headscarved women sitting behind school desks. There is a silence, all heads turn towards me, and then there is a cheerful cacophony of questioning voices. I feel embarrassed to interrupt the class and step back, but Aysel swings the door wide open and invites me in. I sit down at one of the tables. On the wall are posters of Koran texts, and on the blackboard a beamer projects a Koran verse that they were apparently discussing when I entered.

The women are all middle-aged and older. To me, they look no different from the elderly Turkish ladies I know from the Netherlands. I do not understand a word they say, but Aysel translates with the little German she knows. The women expectantly ask me if I am from Germany, because nearly all of them have sons or husbands who work there. Their children have left home, their husbands work or are retired. The domestic obligations are a lot less heavy, so now they can do what they have always wanted to do: immerse themselves more into the study of Islam. That starts with learning Arabic, and then the reading of the Koran, verse by verse.

I look at the screen. The text projected is verse 2:173, or the 173rd verse (*aya*) of the second chapter (*sura*) of the Qur'an. It names what is forbidden (*haram*) to eat, adding that the prohibition does not apply in cases of emergency, such as hunger, or if the forbidden food is consumed by mistake.[5] In an impulse I ask Aysel if she could be so kind as to show verse 4:34. She looks surprised, and I see her frown, but she taps her laptop and the verse appears on the screen.

It is the famous – or should I say infamous – verse saying that men oversee women and that they may admonish or even beat them if the women disobey their husbands.[6] No wonder Aysel does not think it

---

5 In the English translation of the Qur'an by Hilali and Khan, this verse reads as follows: 'He has forbidden you only the maitah (dead animals), and blood, and the flesh of swine, and that which is slaughtered as a sacrifice for others than Allah (or has been slaughtered for idols, on which Allah's Name has not been mentioned while slaughtering). But if one is forced by necessity without wilful disobedience nor transgressing due limits, then there is no sin on him.'

6 In the English translation of the Qur'an by Hilali and Khan, this verse reads as follows: 'Men are the protectors and maintainers of women, because Allah has made one of them to excel the other, and because they spend (to support them) from their means. Therefore the righteous women

appropriate for this group of women. But I have a special interest in this verse. For years, I taught a class where the students were asked to come up with the best translation of this verse, using all kinds of dictionaries, exegeses, legal texts and modern interpretations. And every time it turned out that the text was not at all as unambiguous as is often assumed. For example, one of the translations is that men are 'the protectors' of women, but the Arabic term for this can also be translated as 'custodian' or 'guardian' or 'partner'. The traditional interpretation of the verse had been that men have *authority* over women. According to some interpretations, however, this verse is about the *responsibility* that men have for women. That is quite something else. Proponents of these kind of interpretations are often referred to as 'Islamic feminists'. These feminists also argue that the terms 'obedient' and 'beating' are incorrect translations of the Arabic. Some translators of the Qur'an nowadays feel the need to make these nuances of interpretation clear in their translations.

The women look pleased when I tell them this. Aysel stares at me quizzically while her students are engaging in a lively conversation about this verse. I do not know what possesses me to do this. Why do I have to breach the religious conservatism of these countrywomen with the latest views of Islamic feminism? But I have no time to think about it because the door suddenly swings open and a bulky man in his fifties steps inside. It is the imam who is checking on all that noise. Aysel hastily switches back to the previous Qur'an verse on the screen and introduces me to the imam. We exchange pleasantries, and then I take my leave.

---

are devoutly obedient (to Allah and to their husbands), and guard in the husband's absence what Allah orders them to guard (e.g. their chastity, their husband's property). As to those women on whose part you see ill-conduct, admonish them (first), (next), refuse to share their beds, (and last) beat them (lightly, if it is useful); but if they return to obedience, seek not against them means (of annoyance).'

CHAPTER II

THE MUFTI OF KOMOTINI

The sharia court in Komotini is a small complex of buildings plastered in pastel pink and arranged in a U-shape around a courtyard: a mosque on the left, the offices of the judge and the clerks at the far end and the court on the right. The courtyard, where a small corner is set aside for old Ottoman tombs, is separated from the street by a gate.

The court complex is an oasis of calm in the hustle and bustle of the shopping streets that enclose it. The street in front of the entrance gate is lined with shops that seem ancient, with hand tools, carpets, copper and zinc pots and baskets with spices displayed on the pavement. On the other side of the complex, behind the mosque, is a more modern-looking shopping street with air-conditioned shops selling fashionable clothes, electronics and stylish spectacles. I am too early for my appointment with the mufti, so I drop in at one of the many coffee shops that have chairs outside under a canopy. The summer morning sun is already making itself felt. From behind my cappuccino I watch the people passing by.

The Muslim community of Thrace is divided into three regions, each with a religious leader, the mufti. In the Islamic tradition this is the name for any scholar who, on request, provides a ruling (*fatwa*) on issues of Islamic law or theology. But in Ottoman tradition, the mufti was also the highest clerical authority of the state, who had the last word in religious matters. The mufti became a function rather than a certain practice of scholarship. The muftis of Thrace follow this Ottoman tradition. But they have also been given two additional tasks: one relates to being *qadi* (judge) in family and inheritance matters and the other to being a representative of the community. It would gradually become clear to me how complex this threefold job description actually is.

The three Thracian muftis are not people who can be found in the telephone book or on the internet. How do I get in touch with them? Even my Greek colleague Angeliki Ziaka, who has an extensive network in the Thracian Muslim minority, had never spoken to them. But she put me in touch with Ioannis Androutsos, who acts as a legal advisor on Greek law for the mufti of Komotini. After some exchanges by email he was willing to make an appointment for me with the mufti.

And so, that morning, I make my appearance at the sharia court of Komotini. At the appointed time, I hesitantly enter the courtyard. People walk past me on their way to and from the mosque or the office but hardly look at me. Then a blonde man in his thirties approaches me. 'I am Ioannis. Welcome!' He accompanies me up the stairs to the vestibule that leads to the clerks' office on the right and to the mufti's office on the left. I want to take off my shoes, but noticing that nobody else does, I keep them on. Ioannis opens the door to the mufti's office and I step inside.

The mufti rises from behind his desk. He is a short old man, dressed in black trousers and a white shirt, with a long black overcoat that reaches down to his ankles. He wears a red fez, around which white linen is draped in the shape of a turban, just like those I know from imams and scholars in Syria and Lebanon. Slightly stooped by age, he stretches out both his hands and pronounces the Arabic greeting: '*Ahlan wa sahlan, marhaban bik!* – Come in, come in, you are welcome!' I do not speak Turkish or Greek, but I do speak Arabic and since the mufti had studied in the Saudi city of Medina, we agreed to communicate in that language.

The mufti shows me a place on the bench under the window, close to his desk, where a man who introduces himself as Mehmet is already sitting. He teaches Islamic theology in Thessaloniki after he finished hisstudies in Saudi Arabia. He follows our conversation with great interest. From time to time, he will act as interpreter, because the mufti's Arabic is somewhat rusty. Next to Mehmet is a man who says nothing during the entire conversation but gets up every now and then to fetch tea and whom I later recognize as the mufti's driver. Ioannis slumps in the only chair in the room and busies himself with his mobile phone.

Why would Muslims go to an Islamic court if they have the choice not do so? One would think they would not, especially if they were women. Even the most religious Muslim woman knows that her position in Islamic law is considerably worse than that of the man. She can divorce her husband only with his permission, cannot marry a non-Muslim man (the Muslim man, on the other hand, can marry a Jewish or Christian woman), inherits a half less than her brother and the man is the head of the family. If you had a choice and were a woman, you would not choose that, would you?

The Molla Sali case was about that very issue: choice. According to the Greek Court of Cassation, the Thracian Muslim minority had no choice, and Islamic law was mandatory for them in matters of family and inheritance law. That was laid down in the treaty with Turkey a hundred years ago. Molla Sali contested this. And while the European Court of Human Rights still had to decide on this matter, the Greek parliament had already passed a law that gave the Muslims in Thrace the choice to settle issues of family law before either a Greek civil court or the sharia court.

I put this issue to the mufti: now that there is a choice, would not every Muslim in Thrace go to the Greek courts and thus put the sharia court out of business? The mufti shakes his head. 'Actually, that choice already existed for years, and Muslims have already been going to the Greek courts. But most people still come here. They live their lives according to the rules of Islam, the sharia, and therefore they also want to solve their problems according to Islam.'

I have been trying for years to find out how this works, this problem-solving with Islamic law. I have visited family courts in Egypt and Syria, read academic research about Islamic family courts in Yemen, Morocco, Iran, Pakistan, Malaysia and Indonesia, and I am familiar with the controversial practices of the English *sharia councils*. During this first conversation with the mufti, which lasts almost three hours, we discuss all the issues of Islamic marriage and divorce.

We begin with Islamic marriage. This is not very different from civil marriage as we know it in Europe: it requires offer and acceptance from the bride and groom ('will you marry me?' – 'yes, I will') in the presence of witnesses. The presence of an imam is not formally required, but traditionally he presides over the conclusion of the marriage. This is something that is often misunderstood in Western Europe, where the mindset is still a mixture of Christianity and Napoleonic law. The Christian perspective shows in the assumption that the role of the imam is pivotal, even constitutive, for the validity of the marriage, just as that is the case for the Catholic priest and, to a lesser extent, the Protestant minister. The Napoleonic perspective is that only a civil marriage is valid before the state and that religious marriages can be performed only after the civil marriage has been registered. Recently, some West European countries, in their effort to ensure that Islamic marriages are first registered as civil marriages, had called in the remnant rule of Napoleonic law, namely that a clergyman who concludes a religious marriage before it has been registered as a civil marriage is committing a criminal offence.[1] But since the imam is, effectively, not concluding the Islamic marriage, but merely presiding over it, this provision of the law has no effect at all. However, I have the impression that these finer points of Islamic law are not known among the Muslims in Europe, so this particular and ancient rule of criminal law does seem to have some deterrent effect.

The Islamic marriage is therefore not unlike a civil marriage, the only difference being that the witnesses to an Islamic marriage must be Muslim. This requirement had caused me trouble years ago in Cairo when I was asked to serve as a witness to the marriage of Egyptian friends. They were not religious and did not want any festivities, and they thought it sufficient to restrict the ceremony to simple formalities at the Egyptian Registry Office. I had the strong impression they were eloping, because not even their parents were present. We sat in a small office of the civil registry, and the civil servant went with a bored face through all the formalities checking

---

1 For example: Art. 449, Para. 1 of the Dutch Penal Code; Art. 433, Para. 21 of the French Penal Code. Similar articles can be found in Belgian, Spanish, Italian law.

the identities of the bride, groom and their two witnesses. He checked my passport, but my being a foreigner was apparently no obstacle to serving as a witness to an Egyptian marriage. In a monotonous voice he went through the list: 'Civil status? Address? Religion?' But when I answered I was Christian, he looked up: 'Only Muslims are allowed to act as witnesses at Muslim weddings,' he said admonishingly. My friends protested that they did not want a religious marriage but a civil one. The official was adamant: according to Egyptian family law, there was no such thing as a civil marriage. Muslims could only have a Muslim wedding, which had to be registered at the civil registry. And for that Muslim marriage to be valid , Muslim witnesses were needed. Quick phone calls were made to round up another friend who was Muslim and who could drop by the registrar's office at short notice.

Controversial in Islamic marriage law is the age of the bride. Prophet Mohammed married Aisha when she was nine years old, and this is sometimes cited in traditional and tribal Islamic settings today as a justification for child marriages. Although most Muslim countries have signed international conventions setting the age of marriage at 18, they are not always able to control practices in remote areas. According to some Greek studies, such was also the case in mountain villages in Western Thrace. This seemed to be confirmed by the commotion caused in Germany not so long ago when a Greek Muslim from Western Thrace wanted to bring his fifteen-year-old wife to Germany. As it turned out, the marriage had been legally concluded under Islamic law in Greece but was forbidden in Germany because the wife was underage. German commentators clamoured about Muslims performing child marriages.

The mufti remembers this case well, having performed this marriage himself. However, as he explains, it was not just any marriage but a solution to a difficult situation. The girl had become pregnant at the age of fourteen and wanted to marry the father of her child, but Greek law did not allow this because she was underage. The problem was that she came from the Muslim Roma community, where abortion as well as illegal children are unacceptable. But equally unacceptable was being an unmarried mother. The girl therefore ran the considerable risk of becoming a victim of honour killing. The help of the mufti was sought, and he came up with the solution: Islamic law allows the marriage of a girl as soon as she is sexually mature. Through marriage, the honour of both the girl and the community could be saved. When the German commotion reached the halls of Greek parliament, and some members vilified the 'backwardness' of the Muslim communities in Thrace and criticized the lack of human rights, a West Thracian parliamentarian retorted with the rhetorical question: 'Is a dignified life for this girl not a more important human right than the age of marriage?' But human rights lawyers were quite upset about this situation. Ioannis admired the mufti's ingenuity but felt uncomfortable with the solution: 'It has put Greece in a very bad light.'

An issue in Islamic marriage and divorce that creates controversies time and again is the bridal gift. This is a sum of money that the groom gives to the bride at the wedding. Strictly speaking, it is not a bridal price (the amount of money that the groom gives to the bride's father in exchange for marrying off his daughter), nor is it a dowry (the trousseau that the bride takes to her marital home). No, this is a sum of money to be paid by the husband to the wife. And it is her personal property, which the husband is not to touch.

However, according to custom, the amount of the bridal gift is mentioned in the marriage contract, but payment of it takes place only when the marriage ends, that is, with the death of the husband or at the time of divorce. Legally speaking, it is a deferred payment. Some Islamic legal scholars therefore consider the bridal gift as a form of alimony: if the man wants to divorce his wife, he will have to pay this amount to his wife, which will then serve as alimony after divorce. Other legal scholars see the bridal gift as a last resort against a rash divorce: the man will think twice before divorcing his wife if it means he has to pay up a significant sum of money. But many activists and feminists see it mainly as a symbol of the subordinate position of the woman in Islamic marriage law. To them, this bridal price is nothing more than an ordinary purchase price paid by the husband to buy his wife.

Regardless of how one looks at it, the controversies of the bridal price often offer interesting glimpses into the social structures of the people involved. In the United Arab Emirates, for example, there was an increasing tendency since the 1980s of men marrying foreign women. The Emirati women complained about this: since they were, by law, not allowed to marry foreign men their only available partners were Emirati men, but there were ever fewer of them owing to their preference for foreign partners. The men justified their choice of marriage with the argument that the Emirati women demanded exorbitant sums for their bridal gifts. The men could just not afford such sums. The women countered that they had little choice in the matter: in their culture, the amount of the bridal gift is a sign of prestige and respect, and in the wealthy Emirates such as Dubai and Abu Dhabi, these amounts were logically higher than might be expected elsewhere. Both parties appeared to have reached a deadlock. Finally, the government stepped in and established a fund from which men from the United Arab Emirates could receive an allowance for their bridal gift if they married an Emirati woman.

For some Muslim women this is a disgraceful spectacle. After the Algerian War of Independence, in 1962, for example, women called for the abolition of the bridal gift. They had fought side by side with the men for the liberation of their country, and they thought it inappropriate that this equality in wartime was being undone in peacetime by something like the bridal gift. Although the women made their point clear, the complete abolition of the Islamic rule of the bridal gift was considered a bridge too far. The compromise was to maintain the bridal gift but to replace its monetary content with a symbolic gift, such as a Koranic verse recited by the groom.

This may sound like an elegant solution, but the woman who agrees to that may end up penniless at the time of divorce. This is because Islamic divorce law knows no alimony, and after divorce the woman gets only what is her property. If she has not worked and everything has been bought with her husband's money, then she has nothing at all. The bridal gift thus fulfils a certain function in the unbalanced legal relationship between the man and the woman in Islamic family law. Only women who are economically independent can afford the dignified rejection of the bridal gift.

There are not many such women in Western Thrace. In the social relations of the Thracian countryside, the bridal gift still plays an important role. I am told that the customary sum is around 20,000 euros. By Thracian standards that is a large sum of money that will support a divorced woman for about two to three years. But it is not an alimony for the rest of her divorced life. (The alimony for children after divorce is not included in this: that is an ongoing duty that rests on the husband until the children have reached the age of maturity.)

It all becomes even more problematic when the husband does not have the money to pay the bridal gift at all. I am told that this is not uncommon in Western Thrace. On the one hand, this means that the husband will not easily file for a divorce. But on the other hand, the mufti tells me, once such a divorce is initiated, the payment becomes a problem. 'The bridal gift is a suitable instrument in the system of Islamic law, but it is difficult to implement in our society. We live in a society of great poverty; who can pay such amounts?'

This may be advantageous to women who do not want to be divorced but is problematic for women who do want that divorce and at the same time hope for payment in full of the bridal gift. There have been quite a few court cases where women insist on their right to receive payment of the bridal gift in the event of divorce but where the man is unable or unwilling to pay it. The mufti raises his hands in a helpless gesture: 'I do not have the means to force the man to pay. But as long as he does not pay, I cannot pronounce a divorce, because according to Islamic law, that is only possible if the issue of bridal gift is settled. I have no option then but to refer their case to the Greek civil court. They pronounce the divorce according to Greek law, and that is without the bridal gift. So either way, the woman loses.'

But that is unjust, I remark. The mufti shrugs his shoulders and smiles resignedly: 'That's how it is. The woman doesn't get what she is entitled to. If she insists on both her wish to divorce and payment of her bridal gift, and the man can't or won't pay, I cannot pronounce a divorce. If she really wants the divorce, she is forced to give up her right to the bridal gift. That is the harsh reality.'

Our conversation is interrupted by a noise at the door. It opens and the clerk ushers in a young man with an anxious look on his face. He and the mufti get into a deep conversation, with the mufti questioning him in a friendly but pointed manner. Mehmet translates for me. The man's wife gave birth this morning, and the baby turned out to have a kidney problem and was hurriedly admitted to the hospital in Thessaloniki. But the young family has no money to pay the 200 euro admission fee. Can the mufti help? The mufti hardly needs to think and pulls out his wallet, counts four 50-euro notes and gives them to the man: 'Take this and go with God. We will collect it tomorrow during the Friday sermon.' Then he turns to me: 'Where were we again?'

I now turn to the issue of divorce. Under Islamic law, the man may divorce his wife without giving any reason – a legal form of dicorce known in English as 'repudiation'. The woman, on the other hand, is dependent on others if she wants a divorce. She can ask her husband to exercise his right to divorce, often in exchange for her relinquishment of his obligation to pay the bridal gift. What is much better – and what I always advise all Muslim women in the Netherlands – is for her husband to transfer his right of divorce to her by proxy. In that way they both have the right to divorce. But in both instances she is dependent on her husband: if he refuses, it does not happen.

But the most common way for the woman to obtain a divorce is to apply to the judge (provided, of course, she lives in a country where Islamic family law is applied by the court, which is not the case in Europe). The judge can pronounce the divorce if the woman can prove one of the legal grounds for divorce (for example, that the husband does not support her or causes her harm or is sexually inadequate). But in this case the woman is also dependent on someone else – the judge – to get her divorce.

In Komotini, I discover that there is an interesting intermediate form. When I ask whether the husband can indeed use his right to divorce his wife according to his own whims or wishes, the mufti answers sternly: 'The husband has to have really good reasons before I grant the divorce.' This surprises me because the judge has no such authority according to Islamic law: the divorce is the right of the man alone, and he can exercise that right without the permission of others, including the judge. The judge has a say in the matter of divorce only when the woman appeals to the court. But in Western Thrace, the mufti apparently has given himself the right to refuse the repudiation by the husband if he sees fit to do so.

This goes beyond the intervention as practised by most Islamic family courts in the Muslim world. In cases of divorce, whether initiated by the man or the woman, the courts often suspend the proceedings by calling for mediation. Mediation is a well-known concept in Islamic law, and in the case of divorce the judge will appoint family members to act as mediators. These mediators then report back to the judge. If the marriage cannot be salvaged, then divorce is unavoidable. Sometimes mediation is not an option, as is often the case in Western Thrace, where women find that their husbands have gone to work in Germany and started a new family life there.

And what about domestic violence, I ask as casually as possible. Is that a reason for women to file for divorce in Western Thrace? I remember a BBC recording of a hearing in an English *sharia council* in which the woman complained that her husband was beating her, to which the chairman of the *council* remarked that 'some beating' should be tolerated by the wife in marriage.[2] Muslim scholars who hold this point of view justify it with a literal reading of the verse from the Qur'an that I had asked the students of Aysel to have a look at. Does it not say that the husband has the right to 'beat' his wife in case of disobedience? I mention this to the mufti, but he reacts angrily: 'The husband may not hit his wife, ever!' He explained that the word 'beating' in the infamous Qur'anic verse should be read as a tap on someone's arm with a maximum of three fingers. 'The Prophet himself has said that!'[3]

---

2 *See* the BBC recording on YouTube: www.youtube.com/watch?v=rI4W1kgBx2A.
3 I have not been able to find this *hadith* (statement of the Prophet).

Another round of tea is brought into the room. I know I am overstaying my welcome, but it is my only chance to hear the mufti out on all these matters, and I do not know if there will be another opportunity to speak to him. At the same time, I can see that all the talking has made him tired. Maybe it is my turn to tell him about the experiences and views in my part of Europe, so that he can rest and drink his tea.

I tell the mufti that in all other European countries the state recognizes only a civil law of marriage and divorce. Of course, people are free to conclude marriages in accordance with the rules of their religion in their church, mosque, temple or synagogue, but these have no validity before the state or the court. Whatever rules the religious communities want to apply to family matters is their own private affair. And, yes, in Spain a religious marriage can be registered as a civil marriage, clergymen in Scandinavian countries can obtain a licence to conduct a civil marriage, and the United Kingdom allows civil marriages to be concluded in places of religious worship. But in all European countries the overall rule is that a state will recognize only a marriage that is registered as a civil marriage and that the court will only apply civil law to that marriage.

Most believers, whatever their faith, combine the two: they conclude their marriage before a civil registry in accordance with civil law and also within their religious community in accordance with their religious law. This parallel situation has led to a particular problem for Jewish and Muslim women who are married in both systems. They can easily obtain a divorce from the civil court, but there is an obstacle if they also want to endorse this divorce in accordance with the rules of their religion. In Jewish and Muslim law, only the man has the right to divorce. If he refuses – and he can do so without any justification – the marriage stays intact in the eyes of that religion. There are cases known of Jewish and Muslim men who refuse to grant the religious divorce out of spite or because they feel wronged by the civil divorce. For a Muslim or Jewish woman who is devoutly religious, this poses a problem because without a religious divorce she cannot remarry in a religious manner. For Muslim women in European countries there is also another problem. If such a woman comes from a country where Islamic family law applies, and she were to remarry in the European country under civil law without having her religious marriage dissolved, she risks a prison sentence for bigamy when visiting her country of origin. Legal experts have a term for this situation: 'marital imprisonment'. The Jewish term *agunah* is also used: 'caged woman'. The woman is stuck in a religious marriage from which she cannot escape. In some European countries the court has opened this cage with the argument that the husband's refusal for no apparent reason to grant his wife a divorce constitutes an act of tort.

The mufti has listened intently. 'For us, Muslims, the divorce before the Greek court is equal to the divorce under Islamic law. And the reverse is also true: if my court pronounces a divorce, it is also valid in civil law.' In other words: two birds are killed with one stone. That is the advantage if the Islamic and civil courts have the same status. But in most other European countries this logic does not apply. There, civil and religious law are two parallel but distinctly separate systems.

I think I have exceeded the limits of hospitality. I look at Ioannis, who understands my meaning. He stands up, walks to the mufti and speaks to him softly. The mufti nods and rises from behind the desk. 'Will I see you tomorrow?' I would not have dared to hope for that. I gratefully accept the invitation. Together with Ioannis I say goodbye to the mufti and the others in the room, leave the building and cross the courtyard to the exit.

I sit down with Ioannis in the same coffee shop as this morning to recap my discussions with the mufti. Among the many observations that are on my mind I start with one that has nothing to do with law: the mufti speaks Turkish with the people around him, Greek with officials and Arabic with me, but with Ioannis he spoke something else. Ioannis laughs: 'The mufti is Pomak, and I speak a language related to that.' So Ioannis is not Greek? 'Of course I am,' he answers defensively. 'But I am originally from the border area between Greece and the country that is now called North Macedonia; you may have heard about all the fuss there is about the naming of that country.' In that region some people still speak a Slavic language that they themselves call Macedonian. Many Greeks find that highly problematic. If any language can be considered Macedonian, it should be Greek. It is one of the remnants of the bitter struggle about Greek identity. Ioannis sips his coffee and shrugs: 'So that Slavic language is closely related to the Pomaki language that the mufti speaks.' That is all he will say about it.

In the Muslim world, the position of women has been on feminists' agendas for over a century. The feminists – men as well as women – might be believers or non-believers, but their feminism was at first strictly secular. Since the 1980s a new trend, called 'Islamic feminism', has gained popularity. These feminists use Islamic arguments to oppose the subordinate position of women in Islam. They refer to role models like the Prophet's first wife, Khadija, a wealthy widow who headed one of the larger trading houses in Mecca, who had employed Mohammed and who had asked him in marriage. It is a powerful image, which strengthens many Muslim women in their conviction of Islamic equality between men and women. However, in the centuries following the Prophet's death, Islamic law developed a marital system in which the woman's independence is limited to her own properties and her husband has control over her maintenance and freedom of movement. The Islamic feminists dismiss these rules as being contrary to the original idea of Islam. But even if their arguments are theologically valid, it will not change overnight an Islamic law that has been shaped over centuries. That is a battle that will continue for some time.

In Western Thrace, these views have not yet penetrated. The mufti follows the rules of Islamic law, without any novel ideas. But in his rulings, he clearly makes an effort to accommodate the women by applying the rules as broadly as possible. Islamic law does indeed allow for a certain degree of interpretation. But the bottom line is clear: men and women have different rights, and this distinction is most of the time not to the advantage of women. This is not typical of Islamic law. The inferior position of women is inherent in all religious marriage laws. And that is what makes the question I keep wrestling with so poignant: why would women willingly choose such a law when there is also a civil law in which the rights of men and women are equal?

I put that question to Selin, a young Thracian Muslim woman of twenty-eight years. I meet her at the editorial office of the local newspaper where she works part-time as a translator of Greek and Turkish. Turkish is her mother tongue, and although she speaks Greek fluently, it is her second language. We communicate in English, and she deftly navigates any language obstacles with the help of the translation app on her smartphone. She is the first of her family to study at a Greek university. To do so, she had to move far away from home. But she returned with the firm conviction that Muslims and Christians can build a society together in Thrace. 'For me, Islam is very important. But I find religion to be something that is mainly inside. I know I don't follow all the rules, because I sit here outside in the sun with bare shoulders and in public without headscarf. But many of us, the young generation, have more important things on our minds. We have to learn Greek, study, find a job. That is more important than religion now.'

However, some Thracian youth are very religious, sometimes even more religious than their parents. This increase in religiosity is a development that one can also observe among Muslims elsewhere in Europe. 'But it is something that belongs to them personally. They don't impose it on others.' Selin tells me how during her pregnancy a very religious colleague had given her a book called *The Islamic upbringing of your baby*. 'I thanked her but also said that I am raising my baby in love and that religion comes second.'

Selin is content with the way she deals with religion although she finds herself falling short of being a good Muslim. I do not share her self-reproach. She does not drink alcohol, does not eat pork and fasts during Ramadan. And she contracted her marriage at the sharia court. 'It is very important to me that my marriage is Islamic,' she says firmly. But would she also go to the sharia court for a divorce or custody or inheritance? She thinks for a moment and then says decidedly: 'I realize that sharia is a part of our religion, but those rules are very disadvantageous to women. And that is not acceptable in a modern society.'

I pursue my line of questioning: would she, as a Muslim woman, allow herself to marry a Christian man? She and I both know that this is forbidden by Islamic law. The mufti had been very clear about this: 'A Muslim man can marry a Jewish or Christian woman, but not the other way round.' Selin hesitates. 'I think everyone should make their own choice, but I wouldn't do it because my religion doesn't allow it.' She smiles: 'I realize that it may sound strange that I first speak out against the disadvantaged position of women and then support a rule that is actually disadvantageous to women. But that is how it is.'

Now that she seems willing to answer my questions so honestly, I become bolder: if most rules of sharia law are unfavourable to women, would it not be better to abolish the sharia court altogether? Again, she hesitates, stares into her coffee for a while, before saying resolutely: 'When it comes to the functions of the mufti as the leader of the community and as someone who explains Islam for us, then I absolutely think we should have such a person. But as a judge, no, I do not think such a function is needed. For that I might as well go to the Greek court.'

The presence of a parallel justice system of civil and religious family courts that are both recognized by the state may sound absurd to European ears but is quite common in other parts of the world. Some countries do not even have civil law in family matters but only religious law, whereby religious communities have their own laws and sometimes even their own courts. In the case of the Middle East, for example, Syria has one Islamic family law, one Druze, eleven Christian and two Jewish, and each of these communities has its own court. Egypt has one Islamic, six Christian and two Jewish family laws, but all these laws are applied by one single family court (the judge must ask the parties what their religion is to determine the applicable law). Israel has one Islamic, one Druze, four Christian and two Jewish family laws. None of these countries have a 'civil law' that might be used as a neutral option if someone does not want religious law applied. And often the religious communities do not *want* such a civil law. I have always found this very strange: why stubbornly stick to a religious family law that discriminates between men and women? The reason became clear to me during a heated discussion

I had with an Arab lawyer in 1998. She had studied law in Europe, practised law in Kuwait and travelled the Middle East to inform women of their rights under Islamic family law.

The discussion started pleasantly enough in the coffee corner of a chic hotel in Damascus where the lawyer was staying during a lecture tour about family law. We started off as lawyers with a common interest in the legal intricacies and technicalities of Islamic family law. Then she asked me about the family law of Jews and Muslims in Europe. When I replied that almost all European countries apply a single civil law to all citizens, she was shocked: 'What, they don't have a right to their own religious family law? But that is against religious freedom!' I responded that the freedom of religion allows all Europeans to live according to their religious rules in the privacy of their homes and places of worship but that the principle of equality demands that the same family law applies to all citizens of a country. And believers are perfectly free to conclude religious marriages if they want to, but the state courts only recognize civil marriage. It did not convince her: my argument of equality before the law was at odds with her demand for freedom of religion. Two fundamental rights were confronting each other. This was truly a clash of legal cultures. 'If I were a European, I would take this case to the European Court of Human Rights!' she defiantly ended our conversation. Now, exactly twenty years later, this moment had arrived with the Molla Sali case.

But suppose that civil and religious courts coexisted in a country and one had the option to freely choose between them in the case of family and inheritance law. Would not everyone – especially women – immediately choose the civil court? That seemed quite self-evident to me, but it was clearly not for quite some people. Many Muslims I talk to in Western Thrace do not think so either. The mufti of Komotini had said that Islam is important to many members of the Muslim community and that they therefore prefer to apply Islamic rules in full, even if it is sometimes inconvenient. Selin agrees: 'My parents' generation are farmers and simple labourers. They are very conservative people. For them Islam is a natural part of their existence. So, of course, they go to the sharia court. But for the new generation, like me, who have studied and have seen more of the world, it is really different.'

Yet it is not only illiterate or conservative farmers who opt for religious law; educated people also make that choice. This happens even in other European countries. Religious law and religious courts are not as anathema to European society as may be assumed. Catholics, Orthodox, Jewish and various Protestant communities have their own religious laws and their own courts. For centuries these have been part of the European legal landscape and are still in use, not to the extent as was the case one or two centuries ago but enough to allow these institutions to remain functioning.

The term 'religious court' is misleading because it gives the impression that the rulings of this court have the same authority as civil courts. That is not the case. Exceptions are the Church of England, the Lutheran Church in Finland and four churches (Orthodox, Maronite, Catholic and Armenian) in Cyprus, where the courts belonging to these churches have jurisdiction in some areas of law that is recognized by the state. In the other countries these religious institutions have authority only within the religious community itself. I therefore prefer to use the term 'religious tribunal' rather than religious 'courts' to make clear that they are not part of the state. These tribunals deal with all kinds of religious issues, ranging from acknowledgement of conversion (mostly in in Jewish tribunals) to disputes between the clergy and the faithful (in Protestant tribunals). Most tribunals also adjudicate in cases of divorce.

For Jews the situation of divorce is not unlike that of Muslims: it is the husband who is solely entitled to divorce, not the wife. There is considerable case law from Jewish tribunals in Europe of Jewish wives who ask for a divorce but whose husbands refuse to grant it to them. The problem is that the husband does not have to provide a justification for his refusal and that the tribunal can do nothing about it because it is the husband's God-given right, and he may use it as he pleases. Even a divorce obtained by the wife from the civil court is no reason for the husband to grant her a divorce under Jewish law. This is the situation of 'caged woman' that I had explained to the mufti: she is imprisoned in her Jewish marriage and therefore cannot remarry according to Jewish law.

Under Catholic law the issue of divorce is somewhat easier, because it is simply forbidden. What is possible, however, is that the marriage is annulled. This means that the marriage is declared to have never existed. The nullification is to be decided by the Catholic tribunal. The most common reason given for such nullification is that the marriage was never consummated, that is, the spouses never had intercourse. This sounds a bit far-fetched, but the undoing of an earlier Catholic marriage is critical for the devout Catholic who wants to remarry in the Catholic Church.

Most Protestant denominations take a more pragmatic view of marriage law. In quite a few North European countries their particular kinds of Protestantism historically were – and sometimes still are – so intertwined with the state that these communities consider civil marriage equal to religious marriage. Unlike Greece, where both forms of marriage are valid, the communities consider civil marriage the only valid marriage, complying, as such, with God's regulations. The same is the case with divorce. That makes things considerably easier. That is the reason their tribunals have little work to do in the domain of family law but all the more when it comes to disputes over doctrine or about the appointment of ministers.

The next day I arrive a bit earlier at the sharia court because I want to stop by the clerks' office. The older clerk sits by himself in the room looking over some papers. He gives me a friendly welcome, and we exchange pleasantries in Arabic. He is one of the few in the court who knows Arabic, because he too studied in the Saudi city of Medina, just like the mufti and Mehmet the teacher. And apart from the mufti, he is the only one who knows Ottoman, the language in which the final ruling of every court case is written. He shows me the book with the rulings in Ottoman and the folders with the same rulings handwritten in Greek and Turkish. I do not read any of these three languages, but I can see from the half-page rulings that they do not contain elaborate considerations or references to Islamic law manuals or to articles of law.

The lack of a law book, a code of family law, surprised me at first. Apparently, Western Thrace has not transposed Islamic law into a code of law, as most Muslim countries have done. To be clear, the sharia, or Islamic law, is not originally a book of law either. The sharia consists of a large collection of commentaries on rules derived from the Qur'an (the word of God) and the Sunnah (the words of the prophet Mohammed). These commentaries were written by legal scholars who were more theologians than lawyers. One such scholar could write several commentaries in his lifetime, and these often consisted of several volumes. If one takes into account that this was done over several centuries by legal scholars living in the vast Islamic empire that stretched from Morocco to Afghanistan, one can easily imagine the enormous size of the collection of legal literature they produced through the centuries. That entire collection makes up the corpus known as Islamic law.

The commentaries were so complex and vast that they were not fit to be used as reference in courts of law. A peculiarity of the history of Islamic law is that judges and Islamic scholars were often not – and still are not – one and the same person. Judges were practitioners of the law, not scholarly specialists on sharia law who knew their way in the vast collection of theological-legal literature. When judges had to make decisions on matters that pertained to Islamic law, such as family law or certain forms of criminal law, they consulted the legal scholars. Their interpretation of the Islamic aspects of the case was called a *fatwa*, and the scholar who issued the ruling was for that particular purpose called a *mufti*. In the case of Western Thrace, the two functions of judge and scholar were united in one person. This is a unique situation compared with the rest of the modern Muslim world.

Another unique feature of Western Thrace is that Islamic family law is not codified in a book of law. During the 20th century, this has been done by almost all Muslim countries. It was the result of an urge for modernization. Not only technology but also infrastructure (railroads, post offices) and state institutions (parliament, judiciary) were to be drastically introduced as part of large national modernization projects. That also included the legal system. In particular, Islamic family law was sublimated into a single legal code. Countries like Morocco, Iran, Pakistan and Indonesia each promulgated their own code of Islamic family law. (Interesting detail:

Turkey is one of the few Muslim countries that rejected the use of religious family law and in 1926 opted for a single civil family law.) Although these countries all draw from the same sources of Qu'ran and Sunnah, and from the collection of Islamic commentaries, their laws can be quite different. An important consequence of these codified forms of sharia law is that judges no longer need to seek the advice of scholars: they can refer directly to the articles in the law that are much clearer and more accessible than the complex elaborations of the legal commentaries. As a consequence, the role of the scholars in Islamic law was largely over as there was no need for judges any more to seek the scholars' counsel on issues of Islamic family law.

This, however, was not the case in Western Thrace. With the Treaty of Lausanne, in 1923, the situation of that time has been frozen, as it were, and all the developments of the following century have passed them by. The mufti acts as a judge but has no code of law available to him. He therefore needs to rely on his other role, that of the religious scholar, who bases his rulings on the old commentaries. But does he? On the bookshelves in his office, I do not see any handbooks or commentaries prescribed by the Islamic school of law of the Hanafites, the leading Islamic school of law in South-Eastern Europe and the Middle East. I ask the mufti about this, but his answers are vague. This begs the question of whether he actually consults this literature in his decisions or even whether he is familiar with this literature at all. In hindsight I blame myself for not having pressed this issue with the mufti.

In the rulings recorded in the books and folders that I leaf through in that dusty secretariat there is no sign of reference to any authors or books of the old commentaries. The system of the sharia court in Komotini clearly rests on the trust that both the Greek state and the Thracian Muslims place in the mufti. This lack of procedural transparency has been widely criticized by activists and human rights lawyers. After all, an essential element of jurisprudence is that there should be clarity about the basis on which a court issues its rulings and about the procedures that are used to reach that conclusion.

I am not allowed to attend the court cases of the sharia court. It is confidential, they say. That is a pity, but understandable: in most other countries court cases regarding family law take place behind closed doors. Besides, there are not that many cases. The mufti estimates that each of the three sharia courts handles an average of twenty to fifty divorces a year, plus a few inheritance and custody issues, and disputes about territories that have been placed under religious foundations (*waqf*). There is no overcrowded court calendar, and no long waiting times, as is the case in the civil courts.

The majority of the conflicts and problems that the mufti deals with, however, do not follow the agenda of the court, but are spontaneously submitted to him by people who stand waiting in the vestibule to go in one by one. This shows that the mufti is more than a judge: he is also the spiritual leader of the community and the highest religious authority when it comes to the interpretation of Islam. This is why the conversations I have with the mufti are repeatedly interrupted.

At the end of our second conversation the mufti invites me to accompany him to his home in the village Arranios, 30 kilometres outside of Komotini. This is an unexpected honour, which I accept gratefully. We get up, and while the clerk quickly removes all the paperwork from the desk and puts it in a bag, the mufti walks out with a shuffling stride. I suddenly realize that this man with his sharp mind and charismatic appearance is very old. Ioannis had told me that he is eighty years or possibly older.

We slowly cross the courtyard, where a group of middle-aged women stand waiting. As soon as they see him, they crowd around the mufti and start talking agitatedly. Mehmet, who has accompanied us, translates. One of the women is engaged to someone, but her neighbour who has a crush on her has threatened to harm her if she does not marry him. The women's voices are shrill and panicked. The mufti raises his hand, and the women fall silent: 'Ladies, threats are a matter for the police, not for me. It is best if you report it to them.' And with these words he walks on. The women make way and respectfully murmur their thanks and greetings.

At the gate waits a guard who escorts the mufti to his car. The driver lets the mufti in the back and then gets behind the wheel. Ioannis and I follow in my rental car. We drive out of the city and on narrow roads through the countryside. Ahead of us rise the mountains of the border region with Bulgaria. After a twenty minutes' drive we arrive at a village, where we stop at the mufti's house. He walks ahead to announce to his wife and daughter that male guests are approaching. The word 'male' means that headscarves will be tied and the word 'guests' that tea will be made.

It is a small and simple house with a living room, a kitchen and three rooms. Mehmet, Ioannis and I sit down on the sofa in the living room, and the mufti tells us about his youth and the village where he grew up. His wife puts the tea on the table and joins us. She asks Ioannis to pass the tea around. Suddenly, the mufti stands up: 'I have to show you something.' He walks out of the room and returns with a leather tube about 80 centimetres long. In it is a roll of parchment, which he takes out carefully and then rolls out on the floor. We have to push aside the table and chairs, for the scroll is at least three metres long. The parchment is old – that much is clear – and is filled with names in Arabic script. On one side of the scroll is the name of the Prophet. From there follows a sort of family tree with endless branches that fan out over the entire length of the scroll. These are the names of all the Sufi shaykhs of this region, the mufti tells us.

Sufism is the mystical side of Islam, which was very popular in the Balkans during the Ottoman era. Sufism is practised in *tariqas*, which are a kind of orders led by a spiritual leader who is often called *a shaykh*. I know the term from the Middle East as a form of deference when one addresses an elderly person. But it is also the title of the spiritual leader. Some shaykhs achieved international fame, and their followers came from far and wide, and on the death of a renown shaykh his tomb often becomes a place of pilgrimage. Much later I heard that the mufti was also a Sufi shaykh. But right now, in the living room, he says nothing about it. Together we look at the scroll. I am deeply impressed: here on the floor lies a part of history of this region that is on the verge of extinction. For who will succeed the mufti, who will follow in his footsteps as shaykh and as leader of the community? And how long will the sharia court continue to exist?

VIDEO FOOTAGE

The short video clip *Portrait of a Thracian mufti* and 3D images of the courtroom of the Komotini sharia court and it surroundings can be seen when using this QR code:

CHAPTER III

THE TURKISH DIMENSION

When I do not have appointments in Komotini, I spend my time reading and writing in one of the many coffee shops. It is a small town, but it has a university and that shows. Trendy coffee shops are to be found on every street corner, with young people chatting or working behind laptops. They roll their own cigarettes and are allowed to smoke them inside (I had forgotten how much that makes clothes stink). Pink Floyd, Bob Dylan and Bob Marley are played on the speakers.

The coffee shop around the corner from my hotel has become my regular workplace, and the barista knows how I like my coffee. From the moment I met him, I was fascinated by the tattoo on his arm: the name 'Marie-Elena' written in Arabic script. He is not the only one who does that. I see many Greek youngsters with tattoos in Arabic. Are they Muslim? But no, the barista is called George, which is a typical Christian name, and I had also seen many such tattoos in Thessaloniki. Only after a few days do I dare ask him what it means. He grins sheepishly: 'It's my wife's name. And it's cool to do it in funny characters. I find that Arabic looks nicer than Chinese.'

I regularly speak with him about the community in Komotini. He is a Christian himself and confirms what so many people tell me: Muslims and Christians live together in harmony. Is this really the case, I wonder, or do they want it to be so? After all, it does not seem as though they go to the local discotheque together or have relationships with each other, let alone get married. I do not say this out loud as the barista continues talking while making my coffee: 'The Turkish..., sorry, I mean the Greek Muslims are just like us, and they often come here for coffee as well.' He looks up, as if pondering. 'Only with older people it's different. They hardly speak Greek. I don't understand that, you know, it's just a shame that they don't. Why can't they make the effort?'

Selin has an explanation for this: 'I am the first generation to go to Greek schools and Greek universities. My parents' generation hardly spoke Greek because it was not necessary. Only some of the men spoke a word of Greek if they worked in the factory in town. But most people hardly ever left their village. In fact, until 1994 the people of my village were only allowed to leave with a pass. There were barriers and guards that blocked the roads in and out of the village. And we were not the only one; it was true for more villages.'

Huh?! What kind of story is that? Selin shrugs her shoulders: that was what her parents told her. And no, she does not know exactly why that was either. 'I think it was because the Greeks saw us as a danger, because we are Turkish. And Greece and Turkey have always been enemies.'

When in our next conversation Selin mentions again that Muslims and Christians live harmoniously together in Western Thrace, I cannot help but ask whether this is really the case. 'I'm really not treated differently from anyone else,' she answers. 'But anyhow, they cannot see that I'm a Muslim,' she adds cheerfully, 'because I don't wear a headscarf.'

'And if you say your name when you introduce yourself?' I ask. 'Then they hear that you are Muslim. How do they respond to that?' I think of the many cases in Western Europe where Muslims have been rejected for a job because of their name on their application. She stares into her coffee mug thoughtfully. 'You are right. Sometimes they respond funny. I never wanted to pay attention to that. But yes, it does happen.'

Later on, Selin makes another casual remark that proves to me that the coexistence of Muslims and Christians is not the integrated community that people want me to believe it is. We walk through Komotini on our way to one of the oldest Ottoman buildings in town that Selin wants to show me. She tells me the ancient history of the town where the Ottomans had ruled a century before they conquered Constantinople in 1453. Every five minutes Selin greets a passer-by in Turkish. They are friends and acquaintances, or her students whom she teaches Greek. The building she wants to show me is an *imaret*, a stone building that in Ottoman times was dedicated to the study of the Qu'ran. Because of that pious purpose it is also the place where orphans and soldiers could get free food. It dates from around 1360 AD and is older and much smaller than the one in Kavala. The building does not have an Islamic function anymore and is now a museum of ecclesiastical art.

The building is closed, and I grumble that the sign on the outside wall tells me everything about the collection but nothing about the history of the building itself. Selin shrugs her shoulders: 'People here are not that interested in Ottoman history. We, the Muslims, learn about it in our schools, but not the Greeks, who learn their own history. In that history, the Ottomans mainly play the role of oppressors.'

She says it with a smile, as she would probably do with every startled reaction by someone who, on hearing her name, realized that she was not Christian Greek but Muslim Turkish. It is as if she has unconsciously decided that this kind of situation will not affect her. Living together in harmony requires a positive outlook.

From Komotini, I drive further east to the other town with a sharia court, Didymoteicho, on the Turkish border. It is June, the sun is shining and it will soon be hot. I leave the main road and drive on narrow roads along the tobacco fields that this region is famous for. There is little traffic on these country roads apart from an occasional pickup truck with three or four men and women. They are almost all elderly people, aged over 50. The women wear straw hats over their headscarves. There are few people in the fields: often it is just a man and a woman, a couple I suspect, and they are only more when harvesting the tobacco. It is intensive work: I see tractors driving at a walking pace through the field and behind them, seated on an attached cross-beam, three or four people stooping down to collect the tobacco leaves.

Although the villages look well kept, with sparkling whitewashed walls and orange roof tiles everywhere, and the fields around them look rich and fertile, I keep in mind what everyone has told me: this is not a prosperous region. Almost all the young people have left, first to study in Greece or Turkey, then to work in Germany or at sea, and the elderly stay behind and work the land. Some years ago, when the fasting month of Ramadan coincided with the summer (Ramadan follows the lunar calendar and thus shifts by a week each year), these old people worked their fields in the scorching sun without eating or drinking as long as there was daylight. I am reminded of what the mufti told me: Islam and all its rules are important to these people, including its inconveniences. Skipping or shortening the month of fasting is out of the question. A little bit of Islam is not possible; it is the whole package or nothing.

I open the car windows to let the warm wind blow in, and I think about the issue that kept cropping up in all the conversations I have had so far: the role of Turkey. Turkey was the other party to the Treaty of Lausanne and still acts as the advocate and protector of what they call the 'Turkish minority'. But the same applies, reciprocally, to the relationship between Greece and the Greek minority in Istanbul and Eastern Thrace. Greece and Turkey have, since a century ago, locked themselves in an iron grip of reciprocity, from which they seem incapable to escape.

This shows for example in Turkey's direct involvement in the management of the Turkish-Islamic schools in Western Thrace (just as Greece is involved with the few remaining Greek Orthodox schools in Istanbul). The Treaty of Lausanne stipulates that these minority schools offer their education in 'their own language', and since most Thracian Muslims speak Turkish, their minority schools are Turkish speaking. Therefore, with the approval of Greece, the production of schoolbooks and the training of teachers takes place in Turkey. Shortly after the conclusion of the Treaty of Lausanne the Greek government did try to set up a training programme for the West Thracian Turkish teachers, but the Greek Minorities Inspector prevented this because the training was mainly in Greek: 'If the training is given in Greek, the curriculum will contradict Muslim customs and traditions.'[1] The logic of this statement may sound odd to today's audience, but in the Greek-Turkish context language was

---

1 This statement is quoted in Tsitselikis, *Old and New Islam in Greece*, p. 450.

equated with religion. And religion was protected by the Treaty of Lausanne.

The education at the schools, however, was not entirely in Turkish. By law, Greek, English, history and geography were to be taught in Greek. This may appear as something positive – the children were getting a bi-lingual education! – but it had odd consequences for the staffing of the school. Since religion and language were assumed to overlap – Muslims speak Turkish, Christians speak Greek – the teachers for the courses that were taught in Greek by default also had to be Christian. This was yet another example of how identity was framed in religion as well as language, and each religion was considered to – literally – have its own language. The strict application of these regulations could lead to bizarre situations. There was the case of a Muslim teacher who applied for a job as an English teacher in a minority school. English is one of the subjects taught in Greek, but this teacher had an excellent command of that language too, so there was no problem. Yet the application was rejected. The reason was not language skills but the religion of the applicant: subjects taught in Greek in minority schools were reserved for Christian teachers, and since this applicant was Muslim she was not eligible for the job.

Even though the pupils in the 'Turkish' schools received some classes in Greek, it fell short of the required level to attend Greek secondary school. They therefore went to Turkish-Islamic secondary schools in Western Thrace, and those who wanted to continue their studies went to Turkey. This pattern started to change in the 1990s with a growing need among the Thracian Muslims for an education in Greek. Selin is an example of this change.

Turkey has been following these developments closely for a century and has regularly intervened as guardian of the interests of the Muslim community in Western Thrace. Until thirty or forty years ago, this may have been understandable in the light of those times, but now voices of discontent about the Turkish meddling can be heard among the West Thracians. There is much talk of 'interference' by the Turkish consulate in Komotini. The clearest example of this, I am told, is the issue of the 'elected' muftis: in protest against the muftis appointed by the Greek government, like the mufti I had spoken to in Komotini, part of the Muslim community in Western Thrace took matters into their own hands and elected their own muftis. These elections, and the resulting elected muftis, are supported financially and logistically by the Turkish consulate.

Ibrahim Serif was one of those elected muftis. We had arranged to meet a few days earlier on a terrace in Komotini, where only Turkish is spoken and it was clearly Serif's regular spot, as he was continuously greeted and addressed by visitors. We drank small cups of strong Turkish coffee under the shade of the trees. Serif was a tall, slender man in his early seventies who spoke in a soft voice, the mirror image of the man who accompanied him. He was a stocky fifty-year-old man who spoke in a bellicose tone and began by asking why I had gone to see the appointed mufti first and not this elected mufti. This man would dominate the conversation that afternoon, and I had the distinct impression that he was connected to the Turkish consulate and was here to oversee the conversation with a foreigner. I answered, truthfully, that I had the contact details of the appointed mufti before those of the elected mufti. It was Selin who had arranged this appointment through a friend of the daughter-in-law of the elected mufti.

We bypassed the thorny issues of legitimacy and soon found ourselves in an animated conversation. 'Instead of allowing us Muslims to elect our own religious leaders, the Greek government is forcing them on us,' the consulate man said, defending the initiative of some West Thracians to elect their own mufti. 'And that is also what it says in the Treaty of Lausanne: the Muslim muftis in Greece are elected by the community, just as the Greek Christian community in Istanbul is allowed to elect its own leaders.'

That was indeed what the treaty stipulated, but the Greek authorities took the legal position that the muftis also act as judges, and judges in Greece are not elected but appointed by the state. The mufti of Komotini had other reasons to oppose elections of his function: 'How can people have a good idea of the qualities and skills of the mufti they have to choose?' Selin had reacted strongly when I told her this: 'We are not stupid, are we? We can choose our politicians and administrators but not our muftis?! And if he doesn't do a good job, we'll vote for someone else a few years later – as simple as that.' But the mufti of Komotini was also very scornful of the election process itself: 'They call it "elected" mufti, but I ask you: how was he elected? Did we, Muslims, have elections? No, he was just nominated, and no one dared say no.'

Whatever reasons Thracian Muslims may have to elect their mufti or not, I am slightly puzzled about Turkey's involvement in this. Ever since 1924, Turkey has been a secular state that, like France, wants all forms of religion removed from public life. Headscarves, for example, have been banned from state universities and parliament for almost a century. Admittedly, Erdogan's Islamic policy has recently changed this, but still: why this Turkish support for such a typically Islamic institution as the mufti? Does Turkey genuinely feel responsible for this Turkish minority and hence wants to live up to its commitments under the treaty, as it claims? Or is there some political pragmatism in play whereby the Thracian Muslim community serves as an excuse for Turkey to keep a finger in its neighbour's pie? After all, Turkey and Greece are not the best of friends, to put it mildly.

This is also the reason why the Greek state preferred not to have elections for the position of mufti. Greece is afraid of the influence that Turkey could exert in such elections. The Turkish consulate has long been active in the community and also has a lot of money at its disposal, so this fear is not entirely unfounded. 'But the Greek government is also partly to blame,' Selin responds cautiously, 'because they really don't listen to us, so they shouldn't be surprised if some people then look towards Ankara.'

Not all Turkish-speaking Muslims share this view. Mehmet, the teacher I met in the mufti's study, is very concerned about Turkey's role. 'Its influence is great. Those like me who teach Islam and who say that we are Greeks who just have to follow the mufti who is appointed by the Greek government, we recently received a letter from the Turkish consulate that we are no longer wanted in Turkey. And if there were elections, they would put people like me under a lot of pressure. I am very concerned that they might threaten me with the deportation of my son who is now studying in Turkey.'

Whatever the underlying reasons and motives, the presence of elected and appointed muftis creates confusion in the Muslim community. Whom to believe, whom to follow? Since the late 1990s, the Greek government has realized that it needs to be more proactive if it wants the Muslim community of Western Thrace to become part of Greek society. For starters, they no longer speak of the 'Turkish minority' but of the 'Greek Muslim minority', and the name 'Turkish school' has been replaced by 'Greek minority school'. At the same time, the 'elected' muftis are kept in check: one year and a half after I talked to Ibrahim Serif, in November 2019, he is convicted to 80 days jail for 'usurping authority' because he was leading a Friday prayer in a mosque, a job reserved for state-appointed muftis and the imams nominated by them.

Didymoteicho is a sleepy town in the afternoon heat. It is the third town in Thrace with a sharia court, and its mufti and I had met several days ago in Komotini, when he was on his way to Didymoteicho. He is a young man who had just been appointed mufti. Our meeting in the hotel lobby was brief but pleasant, and he invited me to visit him in Didymoteicho. I thought we had made an appointment, but when I arrive the sharia court is closed and in the deserted streets is no one who could direct me to his house.

    I do not mind as it gives me the rest of the afternoon to criss-cross the Thracian countryside on my way back to Komotini. I want to have a look at the villages that Selin told me about that were locked off from the world and where the inhabitants could only enter and leave with passes. She had mentioned a few to me and I blindly choose the mountain village of Organy, near the Bulgarian border. The road leading to the village is in excellent condition but winds in sharp U-turns along the mountain slopes, so the twenty-kilometer trip takes one and a half hours. Moreover, it is a dead-end road, so I have to take the same road back.

    Like all villages in Western Thrace, Organy is a collection of whitewashed houses with red-tiled roofs, which contrasts beautifully with the greenery of the surrounding forests. Agriculture is practised along the slopes. If the economy was not so bad, this would be an idyllic place, far from the worries of the cities below. There is no sign of the barriers that Selin mentioned. That is not surprising because they date from over twenty-five years ago.

Since Selin had told me about these villages, the image of those barriers had stayed with me. Were those villages really locked off? And why? I had asked around in Komotini, but many of the younger people had no idea it had ever happened or only knew about it from the stories of their parents and grandparents. Like Selin, they had no memory of it because it was before their time. Those who had heard about it were not sure why, but, like Selin, assumed that it was because those villages were inhabited by Turkish minorities.

The answer came when I put the question to the older generation: yes, it really happened, they told me, but, no, it was not about the Turkish minorities but because of the Cold War. At the time, Greece was staunchly anti-communist, and the Greek security service had set up a zone along the mountainous border area with communist Bulgaria to prevent possible cross-border infiltration. Since this area was mainly inhabited by the Muslim minority, they were the victims of those measures.

When I have finally descended the winding mountain road to reach the flat lands below, I cross the south-north motorway to Bulgaria. 'Border: 10 km,' the sign says. The inhabitants of Komotini regularly cross the border to fill up gasoline, because it is cheaper in Bulgaria and only fifteen minutes away. And it takes the Bulgarian tourists only an hour to get to the ferry from Kavala to the holiday island of Thassos. It is a cynical twist of history: only a few decades ago, all Thracian villages on the Bulgarian border were closed because of possible communist influences, and the Thracian Muslim minority was focused on Turkey, while now there is free access to Bulgaria, and Turkey has become selective about which Thracian Muslims it does allow entry. It is yet another change in regional politics, and the Thracian Muslim minority has no choice but to undergo it.

In December 2017, when the Molla Sali case was playing out in Strasbourg, President Erdogan from Turkey came to Greece on a state visit. This was not just a visit from a neighbour. Greece and Turkey have always had a difficult relationship. Greece blames Turkey for four centuries of Ottoman rule. Turkey blames Greece for having taken advantage of Turkey's weakness in 1919 by invading it after its defeat as Germany's ally in the First World War. Greece, at the time, was driven by the idea of a 'Greater Greece' that wanted to bring all areas once inhabited by Greeks back under Greek rule. This led to the Greek-Turkish War of 1919 to 1922, in which Greek troops advanced as far as Ankara, until they were finally driven back by Kemal Atatürk.

It was Atatürk who, from 1923 onwards, established a modern and secular Turkey by dismantling the Ottoman Empire with a series of 'modernization' measures. In 1923 the Turkish Republic was proclaimed; in 1924 the official status of caliphate was abolished; in 1925 the Islamic calendar was replaced by the Gregorian version; in 1926 Islamic law was abolished and Islamic family law was replaced by civil law (in fact, Turkey copied Swiss family law); in 1928 the Persian-Arabic script of Ottoman was replaced by modern Turkish with the Latin alphabet; and in 1938 the headscarf and turban were banned.

All these measures had bypassed the Turkish community in Western Thrace. With the Treaty of Lausanne, in 1923, they acquired Greek nationality, but also rights that predated 1923 and those have remained unchanged ever since. That is why in Western Thrace, Islamic family and inheritance law is still applied, court decisions are written in the Ottoman language, and the relationship with the state is reminiscent of the *millet* system. It is a freeze-frame situation of almost a century ago.

The year 1923 was also the year that Atatürk made peace with Greece and the population exchange took place between the two countries. But it was a cold peace, which then repeatedly threatened to escalate into armed clashes. Many of these conflicts were fought on the backs of the mutual minorities. The principle of reciprocity played a leading role in this. The clash between the Greek and the Turkish communities on the island of Cyprus, in 1964, prompted Turkey to expel a large part of the Greek minority from Istanbul, and Greece, in turn, took discriminatory measures against the Turkish-Muslim minorities in Kos and Rhodes and in Western Thrace.

The old pains and latent conflicts have kept simmering between the two countries ever since. And they continue to keep each other on their toes with small pinpricks. Just before I arrived, Greek soldiers patrolling the Greek-Turkish border had been arrested by Turkey for allegedly crossing over. In response, Greece detained the pilots of a Turkish military helicopter that had made an emergency landing in Western Thrace shortly before. The Turkish Muslims in Western Thrace and the Greek Christians in Eastern Thrace anxiously follow these developments because they know that when blows fall on one side, the other can expect the same kind of blows.

All the more reason, therefore, for both countries to keep their precarious relations as open and positive as possible. This need was certainly felt when I was visiting Western Thrace, because in 2016 the European Union had reached an agreement with Turkey on the reception of the massive Syrian refugee flow that had started the year before. Greece benefited greatly from this agreement, as it was the first European destination of these refugees. All these issues would certainly have been discussed by the heads of government. But Erdogan also took the opportunity to visit the Muslims in Western Thrace.

It was not the first time Erdogan had been to Western Thrace. But this time his tone had become sharper. Earlier, in 2004, when he visited Greece in his capacity as prime minister, Erdogan called on the minority to cooperate with Turkey for the good of Greece, but emphatically did not use terms like 'Turkish' minority. This time was different. During his visit to Komotini, Erdogan made it clear that Turkey was acting as a protector of this minority. He said it was a shame that these Muslims' economic circumstances were disadvantageous compared with those of the other Greeks. And he raised quite a few eyebrows when in his address to the Thracian Muslims he remarked: 'You and we together form one people.'[2]

Still, it is unclear how popular Turkey is with the Muslims of Western Thrace. Their poor attendance at Erdogan's visit may be a clue. Local newspapers reported that the hall in Komotini where

---

[2] His speech is not available in written form, but these words were quoted by a Greek journalist from Thrace who had attended the speech.

Erdogan held his speech was being filled up by busing people in from Turkey.

Turkey is not only important in the ways it conducts its politics towards today's Muslim community in Thrace. It has also left the legacy of the minority system that is still prevalent there. For centuries the Ottoman Empire governed its religious minorities according to the *millet system*. That system is, in turn, a successor of the *dhimmi system* in Islamic law. To better understand what is happening now in Western Thrace, it is good to take a closer look at this system. In doing so, a comparison with the Christian ways of dealing with religious minorities is helpful because most of today's legal systems in Europe are indebted to that particular legacy. Both the Islamic and the Christian systems hinge on the principle of the freedom of religion, but the ways this principle has been shaped have given rise to two radically different legal systems.

Islam has two characteristics that make its dealings with religious minorities different from those of Christianity. The first characteristic is that, since its earliest beginnings, Islam has recognized other religions. Of course, Muslims thought that their religion was the best, but they saw Islam as the successor to Judaism and Christianity and accorded these religions the respect as precursors of Islam. According to Islam, all three religions share the same God and the same prophets that God has sent to mankind to instruct them into His Revelation. Jesus, according to Islam, was not a son of God, but a prophet in a long series of prophets such as Adam, Noah, Abraham and Moses, a series that ended with Mohammed. Later, Muslims would also recognize religions other than Judaism and Christianity, provided they were monotheistic, such as Sabianism in the Middle East and Zoroastrianism in Persia.

The second characteristic is that Muslims have not developed a practice of forced conversion. That did happen, of course, but not on a large scale, and it was never the aim of the Muslims' wars of conquest. The Islamic empire that was established in the first century of Islam (8th century AD) was therefore an empire in which the Muslims were in power, but in which they themselves constituted a small minority. The majority of the empire's population were Christians and Zoroastrians. It was only after two or three centuries that these demographics began to change in favour of Islam: more and more people converted to Islam, perhaps because they believed that this religion was better but more often because being a Muslim provided access to positions of power and meant an exemption from the special taxes that non-Muslims had to pay. In any case, we can see that for a long time the term 'minority' was, strictly speaking, not applicable to the non-Muslims of the Islamic Empire.

These two characteristics formed the basis of what was called the *dhimmi system*: the non-Muslims in the Islamic realm were given the freedom to live according to their own religious rules. This religious freedom included having churches and synagogues and observing religious rituals such as prayer, fasting, baptism, holidays and even the use of wine. Since religion in those times also included everything related to family life, non-Muslims were free to apply the rules of their religious family laws. And so, each religious community decided on its own family law and often had its own court to decide on issues of marriage, divorce, children and inheritance. We have already seen that these religious courts still exist in most Muslim countries that were part of the former Islamic empire.

The flip side of this religious freedom was that non-Muslims suffered a secondary status as citizens of the Islamic empire. Their civil rights were less compared with those of Muslims. The basic rule was that a Muslim could not be subjugated to a non-Muslim. In practice this meant that a non-Muslim could never be in a position of authority over Muslims. A non-Muslim could not bear witness against a Muslim, nor could he be a judge, army general or market supervisor. The segregation between Muslims and non-Muslims was well regulated, although historians have shown that these same rules were continuously used and misused by both communities.

When in the 14th century the Ottomans began their conquests of what is now Turkey and the Balkans, and in the 16th century expanded their territory to the Middle East and North Africa, they applied this system to their non-Muslim subjects. As in the Islamic Empire, the Ottomans were the rulers, but the Christians formed the majority in the European parts of the empire. The Ottomans transformed the old *dhimmi system* into the more political *millet system* that gave non-Muslim communities (*millets*) a large degree of self-government, with their leaders reporting to their Ottoman ruler. An important consequence was that the non-Islamic subjects of the Ottoman Empire did not feel so much 'Ottoman' as primarily Orthodox or Jewish or Catholic.

How different was the situation in Christian Europe. For starters, Christianity did not recognize any other religions except Christianity. From that view, the world was simply divided into Christians and pagans. (The recognition of Judaism was complicated: on the one hand, Christ was a Jew, but, on the other hand, the Jews were regarded as the ones who had called for Christ's death. From the 10th century onwards, the Jews in Europe would be regularly exposed to periods of persecution and expulsion). The second issue – no forced conversion – was not endorsed by Christianity either. Souls had to be saved, by force if necessary. The active conversion efforts of missionaries and the conversion wars waged by kings such as Charlemagne were therefore more typical of Christian Europe than of the Islamic Empire.

For this reason, the Ottoman Empire was renowned among 16th century European Protestants for its religious freedom. The Protestants were well aware that they would enjoy a secondary status if they were citizens of the Ottoman Empire but that they could at least freely practise their religion without fearing persecution or being burned at the stake, as was the case in Europe. When the Dutch Protestants rose in rebellion against their Catholic Spanish overlords in the 16th century, they used the battle cry 'Better Turkish than Papist!' (in other words, better to live under Muslim than Catholic rule).

An exception to the religious intolerance of most European countries was Spain before the end of the 15th century. Until that time, Catholic and Muslim rulers were fighting each other, but in their realms they both practised the relative tolerance of the *dhimmi* system. Under Catholic rule, the Jewish and Muslim subjects enjoyed religious freedom with their own courts and religious laws, just as the Christians and Jews did under Muslim rule. All this changed radically by the end of the 15th century, when the Catholic Kings conquered the last Muslim stronghold of Granada and expelled all Jews and Muslims from Spain. From that moment on, Spain accepted only Catholicism.

At the same time, a completely different history was unfolding on the other side of Europe. In Catholic Poland lived a Muslim minority known as the Lipka Tatars, which was equal in size to the Muslims in Catholic Spain, but, unlike Spain, they were not persecuted or banned. To the contrary, they were allowed to practise their Islam as they saw fit, and they were highly valued fighters in the Polish army. The reason for this different treatment is perhaps the way they had become part of Polish society. Two centuries earlier the Grand Duchy of Lithuania had asked the Tatar tribes that were roaming the Russian steppes to settle within the Duchy in exchange for their warrior skills that were needed for the Lithuanians to both expand their territory and defend it against aggressors. Later, the Duchy merged with Poland into one of the largest European empires.

The tolerant treatment of the Lipka Tatars was an exception to the rule in Christian Europe. Religious tolerance was seriously considered only from the 16th century onwards, when it became clear that Protestantism was not to disappear and that ways of living together had to be found. The form of tolerance that emerged was radically different from that used by Muslims: European Christians developed an individual approach, while Middle Eastern Muslims had adopted the community approach. The individual approach means that having and practising a religion is an individual freedom that must be guaranteed by the state. According to the community approach, however, this freedom is a communal affair: the communities are responsible for the religious welfare of their members, and they enjoy autonomy in regulating that welfare, whereby the state has a care duty towards the community, not its individual members. This difference between the two kinds of tolerance is crucial for our understanding of the situation in Thrace, as well as that of Europe at large, as we will see,

At the time of the Treaty of Lausanne, the communal system of the *millets* was still very much alive, and therefore that model was enshrined in the treaty and has remained unchanged to this day. In the meantime, however, the views on freedom of religion and religious tolerance have changed dramatically in Europe. From a European perspective, the freedom of religion means that any individual may have a religion, change it, give it up or associate with other believers in a 'church', or even establish a new church. In terms of religion, one may do as one pleases, and the state's role is only to ensure that one can enjoy that freedom. If someone were to proclaim herself pope then that person may expect the wrath of Rome, but that person is free to do so.

The Thracian perspective, on the other hand, is not individual but communal. For this, the Thracian Muslims look at the Treaty of Lausanne as the founding document of their community and to the Greek state for the protection of their community freedoms as enshrined in the treaty. These freedoms are religious and legal autonomy, including education and jurisdiction, and all this is to be practiced in the community's language. This explains why Konstantinos Tsitselikis, the human rights professor from Thessaloniki, was so much against these special regulations: 'That is the *millet system*! Surely this is no longer acceptable in this day and age? We have to get rid of that system as quickly as possible and fit in with modern views on human rights.' These 'modern views' that he referred to are based on human rights as individual rights, not as community rights. But Tsitselikis does not advocate a complete abolition of this system. 'I am not against the community structure of the *millet* system per se. I am against any system that is contrary to human rights. If we can find a way to accommodate human rights and this particular communal system in Thrace, then I'm all for it.'

The day before my return to Thessaloniki, I am sitting in my favourite coffee shop writing down my thoughts and impressions. I want to use my findings in Western Thrace in my course 'Islam and Minorities', which I have been teaching at the university for years. In this course we discuss how Muslims and Islam in the past and present deal with non-Islamic minorities and how Muslims and Islam deal with the situation wherein they are a minority themselves. This reverse situation can be found in many places in the world but has become very topical in the case of Western Europe. It definitely gives rise to heated discussions among my students, many of whom are Muslim.

One of my favourite questions is whether religious minorities in Europe are in need of protection (what a religious minority *is* exactly is another discussion that I save for later). Muslim students always unanimously answer with a resounding yes. But when I ask what they mean by protection they often remain silent. I then rephrase my question: what do Muslims, or other religious minorities for that matter, need in order to get the protection they so desperately want? 'More rights', is one of the more common answers. But it is unclear what rights they are talking about, other than those they already have. The rights to organize, manifest or identify oneself politically, religiously, socially or otherwise are applicable in most European countries. So what more do people want?

In 1995 the Council of Europe (not to be confused with the European Council, which is part of the European Union[3]) adopted a Framework Convention for the Protection of National Minorities. Member states have recognized ethnic and linguistic and national minorities, such as Germans in Denmark, Frisians in the Netherlands, Hungarians in Austria and Albanians and Turks in North Macedonia. (It is equally significant that certain Convention states emphatically do *not* recognize minorities, although they obviously exist, such as Basques in Spain, Bretons in France, Roma in Romania, Russians in Lithuania and Kurds in Turkey.) What is significant is that religious minorities are not recognized anywhere. An exception is perhaps Sweden, which recognizes the Jews, but on closer inspection it shows that they are recognized as an ethnic group, not as a religious minority. Perhaps one day this Convention

---

3   The Council of Europe is an organization of countries that aims to uphold democracy, human rights and the rule of law. All member states are also members of the European Convention of Human Rights. The member states include all EU countries, as well as countries like Russia, Turkey and Azerbaijan.

will become relevant for 'Moroccans' or 'Pakistanis' or 'Turks' in Europe, but not for Muslims.

Why is this so? Why is protection given to linguistic, ethnic or national minorities and not to religious minorities? From a European perspective, the reasoning is that the faithful in Europe already enjoy sufficient protection by means of the freedom of religion. This is laid down in constitutions and in the European Convention on Human Rights (the convention under which the Molla Sali case is now being tried). In addition, the faithful in Europe also enjoy the freedom of association that entitles them to engage in organized forms of religion. From the European perspective, therefore, the freedom of religion covers all the protection needed by the faithful both on the individual and on the communal level.

My explanation of this legal framework usually does not satisfy my students' misgivings. Further discussion reveals that the issue is not the legal protection but the *feeling* of protection. Muslims, in particular, do not feel so protected. Nor do Jews. A treaty like that of Lausanne is music to their ears: at least then a government will have spoken out clearly about the existence and rights of the Muslim minority. But when we elaborate the hypothetical situation of such a treaty in Europe, the Muslim students in my class quickly become hesitant. Such a treaty is contrary to their strong sense of individualistic autonomy. They want to be able to manage their religion in their own way. As one Muslim student remarked: 'Nobody is going to tell me what I should believe, not even a mufti, and especially not one appointed by the state!' It is a clear sign of the individualist characteristic of the European notion of religious freedom.

On the way back to Thessaloniki, I pass Kavala and treat myself to lunch in the *imaret* there, which now serves as a hotel. It is a huge building, many times bigger than the *imaret* in Kavala, with dozens of rooms, two restored *hammams*, several courtyards and a small mosque. I meet the owner, a Greek entrepreneur who has renovated the building and transformed the dilapidated building into a luxury hotel. 'I am not the owner,' she corrects me. 'That is the Egyptian state. This *imaret* was built by Mohamed Ali, after he became the ruler of Egypt, as a tribute to his hometown. I only have a long-term lease. But I have the freedom to renovate it as I see fit. At my own expense of course, Egypt doesn't pay a cent, and at the end of the lease, which is in fifty years, they will get back a beautiful *imaret*.'

We drink coffee while watching the orange trees in the courtyard and the sea beyond. Then she tells the story of Presidents Erdogan and Morsi. Morsi is the Egyptian president who was elected after the Arab Spring in 2011 but was deposed by General Sissi in the summer of 2013. 'That was all very undemocratic, of course, but was quite a relief to me. Because Morsi was about to make a deal with Erdogan. Turkey wanted to trade this *imaret* with Egypt, in exchange for an Ottoman building in Alexandria that is still owned by Turkey.'

CHAPTER IV

RETURN TO WESTERN THRACE

In December 2018, six months after my last visit to Western Thrace, the European Court of Human Rights ruled in the Molla Sali case.[1] The widow was proven right in her claim that her husband had the freedom to draw up his will according to Greek law and was not bound by Islamic law, even though he belonged to the Thracian Muslim minority. The Court had reasoned that if several family laws coexist within a single country (this is the system of 'inter-religious law', which exists in the Middle East but not in Europe), people should be able to choose between them.

This judgment was not unexpected. The mufti had already indicated that this freedom of choice in fact existed and the Greek legislature had passed a law regulating this freedom a year before the Court pronounced its judgment. That should have been the end of it. But the Court had taken a detour to reach its decision and, in doing so, had unnecessarily complicated matters. The Court not merely stated that a person should have free choice between Greek and Islamic family law but found it necessary to compare these two legal systems. In doing so, it drew several puzzling conclusions.

The first conclusion was that the widow, Molla Sali, had been discriminated against. Discrimination means that people receive different treatment in a similar situation. That is definitely the case with Islamic inheritance law because it allots different portions to different heirs, and the woman inherits half of what her brother inherits. But in the Greek case the heirs were all women: the widow and the sisters of the deceased. Still, Islamic inheritance law treats them differently: in the Molla Sali case, the widow would receive

---

[1] ECHR 19 December 2018, 20452/14 (*Molla Sali v. Greece*).

one-fourth of the inheritance and her sisters-in-law three-quarters. Discrimination indeed! On closer reading, however, it appeared that the court was not talking about Islamic law as such, but in comparison with Greek law: under Islamic law the widow, Molla Sali, would receive a quarter of the inheritance, whereas under Greek law she would receive the entire inheritance. That was what the Court considered discriminatory. I found that an odd observation because from that perspective *both* laws are discriminatory and disadvantageous to either of the parties. If Islamic law were applied, the widow would have lost out (she would have received one-fourth of the inheritance and her sisters-in-law three-quarters). But if Greek law were applied, the sisters-in-law would have lost out (they would have received nothing at all). The fact that Greek law was more favourable than Islamic law to Molla Sali was the reason why the Court called Islamic law discriminatory. To me, that was more a selective use of perspective than a judicious use of the concept of discrimination.

The Court tried to solve the issue of discrimination by means of free choice between either of the two family laws. But here, also, I found the legal reasoning of the Court not straightforward. Freedom of choice between two legal systems suggests that it works two ways, but the Court's underlying assumption was that this choice was for Muslims only. What if Greeks wanted to opt for Islamic law? That is not as far-fetched as it may sound. In some instances, it may very well be that Islamic divorce or inheritance law is more advantageous than Greek law. But that seemed not to be the issue here. And, indeed, the law that was passed by the Greek parliament a year earlier made it clear that the freedom of choice works one way: only Thracian Muslims had the right to choose between the two legal systems. The Thracian Christians and the rest of Greece had to stick with Greek law. So much for free choice.

It was obvious from the many pages of the ruling that the Court did not feel comfortable with the coexistence of two legal systems within a single country. It was a situation that the judges were clearly unfamiliar with. That explains perhaps why they were so fixated on the discrimination between the two legal systems. I found that surprising. Because two legal systems such as Islamic and Greek inheritance law are, by definition, different and therefore mutually discriminatory. If these two systems were the same, they would not have had to coexist separately; one of them would have sufficed. If several family law systems coexist, as is the case in many countries in the Middle East, it is precisely because they differ from one another.

This clash of legal views was reflected in the confrontation I had with the Arab lawyer twenty years ago: should different communities have the right to apply different legal systems, or do we want everyone to be treated equally? The Court had looked at a system based on differences through a lens that was shaped by equality. No wonder it did not seem to know what to make of it all.

But there was something else with this ruling. It had to do with the way the Court approached the notion of Islamic law. The Court throughout its ruling persistently used the term 'sharia law'. Not 'Islamic inheritance law', which would be more adequate description, but 'sharia law'. That term is as vague as it is ambivalent. It encompasses many domains of rules, ranging from civil law to penal law, from finance to social conduct, from religious rituals to the conduct of the state. For many people it alludes to violent and oppressive practices by the likes of Boko Haram, ISIS, or the Taliban. And sharia as can be seen in the practices today can differ considerably from the classical legal scholarship from centuries ago, just like sharia can be a justification for terrorists and staunch conservatives as well as for those advocating democracy and women's rights. In short, the term 'sharia' makes sense only if one has a clear idea of what the user of that term means by it.

The Court never made the effort to indicate what it meant by 'sharia' and therefore allowed this vagueness and ambivalence to linger. This was not the first time that the Court omitted juridical precision in Islamic law cases. In a ruling of 2003, the Court stated that 'sharia clearly diverges from [the European] Convention [on Human Rights] values'.[2] Nowhere in that ruling had the Court made clear what it meant by sharia. I found this carelessness surprising

---

2 *Refah v. Turkey*, App. Nos. 41340/98, 41342/98, 41343/98, and 41344/98, Eur. Ct. H.R. (13 February 2003), https://per- ma.cc/AYW7-82JP.

coming from a legal institution of this stature. Lawyers are known to be precise in their choice of words and will not allow the use of technical terms, especially of foreign origin, unless they are clearly defined. In its disregard for precision, the Court issued a ruling that included a serious mistake. By considering that 'sharia' was a violation of European human rights values, the Court effectively declared that Islamic rules pertaining to prayer, fasting, contract and land law are also contrary to these values. I am sure that was not what the Court meant, but that was what it ruled.

Was the Court negatively predisposed towards the rules of Islam? Quite a number of legal scholars who closely monitor the Court's case law are of that opinion. From that perspective, the ambiguity of the Molla Sali ruling made more sense.

I call the mufti in Komotini to get his opinion on the ruling. He is no longer there, I am told. Not long ago, the Greek government relieved the muftis of Xanthi and Komotini of their duties with immediate effect, appointed interim muftis with the promise of elections for new muftis and replaced the secretaries and clerks of the sharia courts. This was not a strange decision in itself: the muftis were in their eighties, and their replacement was overdue, and with the announcement of upcoming elections for muftis the Greek government had met the legitimate wishes of Muslims such as Selin and the group around Ibrahim Serif. The election of muftis was also a clever political move towards Turkey, as it removed Turkish objections to the Greek appointment of muftis. And the clean-up of the secretariats did not hurt either, because the administrative support of the courts had long been criticized for its lack of professionalism.

But the two muftis from Komotini and Xanthi were furious: is this how they were being treated after so many years of loyal service? Of course, they understood very well that they were getting too old for their jobs, but their term of office was due to expire in a year's time, so why this sudden dismissal without any notice? Both muftis initiated legal proceedings to challenge the Greek government's decision.

This is all new to me and, frankly speaking, quite unexpected. It definitely makes things more political and complicated. Now each town has three muftis: the dismissed mufti who is contesting his dismissal, the newly appointed mufti who has been told that he is only interim pending elections, and the elected mufti who keeps grumbling that his election is not recognized. My surprise is even greater when I learn that the newly appointed mufti of Komotini is none other than the skinny elderly clerk. Both my questions about the European Court ruling and these developments in Western Thrace are reason for me to return to Komotini once more, in June 2019.

It is a bit strange to see the elderly clerk, who always used to sit so quietly in a corner in the chaotic secretariat, in full regalia with the white turban and a dark blue robe with gold stitching. It is Friday, and I am standing in the middle of the wide courtyard in front of the sharia court. Prayers have just ended in the adjacent mosque, and the square is awash with the faithful leaving the building. When the last ones have left the courtyard, I see the new mufti appear in the doorway of the mosque. He greets me with outstretched arms and kisses me on the cheek. '*Ahlan, ahlan! Min zaman! Kayf haluka?*' – 'Greetings, greetings! It has been a long time! How are you doing?' As with his predecessor, we speak in Arabic.

He holds my arm, and together we walk to his office. First, we have a look in the secretariat, where he had worked as a clerk for ten years. I do not recognize it anymore. Everything is neat and tidy with the desks empty and folders arranged in closed cabinets. The mufti beams: 'All those years I have been annoyed by the mess here. And by the petty corruption.' Apparently, his former colleague, the corpulent clerk, charged small fees for his intercession with the mufti to get cases processed quickly. 'Shameful! Unworthy of a sharia court! It was high time that he was dismissed.'

We move over to the office of the mufti. I still need to get used to seeing him rather than his old predecessor here. He shows me the chair in front of the large desk. He himself does not sit behind the desk but grabs a chair and comes over to sit next to me. It is just the two of us, without Ioannis, Mehmet or the driver. It is actually not surprising that the Greek government has chosen this clerk as its new mufti. He is one of the very few in Thrace with solid theological knowledge, having studied in both Saudi Arabia and Turkey. He is also the only one who knows Ottoman; in his new capacity as mufti, he now writes his rulings himself in the big book because no one else knows that language.

But what about his succession, I wonder. How can he pass on this knowledge? Where will they get the next generation of competent Islamic scholars? It is true that Mehmet teaches Islamic theology at the University of Thessaloniki, but that course cannot compete with those in Turkey and Saudi Arabia. The new mufti shrugs his shoulders: 'We'll see. God will bring us a solution.'

The Thracian students who go abroad to study Islamic theology prefer Turkey, because it is close by and the students already speak the language. Unlike West European intelligence services, this new mufti is not worried about the few Thracian youngsters who go to Saudi Arabia to study Islam. But he does understand the concerns of Western European countries: 'The problem of those young people in your countries is that they did not grow up in an Islamic environment, like we do here, in a family where Islamic values are propagated. Islam is not something natural; they need to get reacquainted with it. And that is why you see that some become very strict and condemn others if they don't do things in the way they think is right.'

He shakes his head. 'I take the Koran as my starting point, which says that dealing with others must be guided by wisdom, good manners and dialogue. Note that dialogue is in third place. First come wisdom and manners. So, dealing with others is mainly about ethics. That has nothing to do with religion.'[3]

The telephone on the desk rings. The mufti answers and speaks Arabic into the receiver. He hangs up and sighs: 'That was a

---

3 He refers to Qur'anic verse 16:25 (in the English translation by Hilali and Khan): 'Invite to the Way of your Lord with wisdom and fair preaching, and argue with them in a way that is better.'

representative from the Sudanese community in Athens. They have someone who has died and must be buried in an Islamic cemetery. Those exist only here, in Western Thrace. We now have to arrange for the transport of the body.'

With the increase in the number of Muslim migrants in Greece, the demand for Islamic burials in Thrace has risen dramatically. I know these discussions about Islamic cemeteries from Western Europe, where deceased migrants of the first generation are often flown back to be buried in their country of origin, while the younger generation wants a grave near their children. But they want that grave to be in an Islamic cemetery. This is not about the burial rituals or the cemetery itself – many cemeteries in Western European countries already provide separate Islamic 'grave sites'. It is about the fact that Muslims, like Jews, want a cemetery that is not cleared away every few years. The bones of the deceased must not be touched.

We talk for two hours, sitting opposite each other in front of the big desk. Outside it is getting quieter: the midday heat has made everyone retreat indoors. I have the impression that the new mufti likes my being here because he is the one who keeps the discussion going. Could it be because he feels lonely in his new position? All this time we have been alone. Apart from the telephone call from Athens, we have had no interruption by a clerk, a friend, or a Muslim who seeks justice.

Finally, he indicates that it is time to go. He has to attend a funeral service. At such services, acquaintances, friends and neighbours join the family, who sit and shake hands for hours. He closes up behind us and walks out across the empty courtyard. Outside is his car with the number plate on which 'moeftiyet Komotini' is written in Greek. Where is the driver, I ask. And where is the guard, who always accompanied the previous mufti to his car? The new mufti smiles: 'They are both gone. I can drive myself.' And the guard was not there for the mufti or for security but apparently had been appointed by the other clerk to prevent beggars entering.

The following day I pay a visit to the former mufti with whom I had spoken so extensively last time and who has now been dismissed. He has invited me to his home. Again, I drive through the fields and villages with whitewashed walls and red roofs. It is all very Greek yet different. One knows that this is a Muslim environment not only because of the minarets that rise up between the houses, but also because of the blind walls of the houses. Unlike the Christian Greeks, family life here does not take place in the streets but in the enclosed courtyards behind the walls.

I ring the bell at the street door, enter the small courtyard and walk to the house, where the wife of the mufti is waiting for me. Like last time, I am taken in by her friendly face and twinkling eyes under the headscarf. I have brought a box of cakes with me, which I offer with two hands to avoid confusion about whether or not to shake hands. But she puts the box down, grabs my face with both her wrinkled hands, puts her headscarved cheek against mine and gives me several kisses through her headscarf. 'How nice of you to come. Welcome, welcome!' Behind her appears Omer, the new assistant and advisor of the mufti. Ioannis had already told me about him. He and I had met briefly on my arrival in Thessaloniki, where he had updated me about the latest developments. Omer is a young man, clean-shaven, with friendly eyes, who laughs at my bewilderment and translates the words of the mufti's wife. He then takes me inside, to the back room, where the mufti is sitting with Mehmet, the Islamic theology lecturer. Our reunion is jovial.

The mufti looks much more fragile and brittle than a year ago. Is that because of age or because he is not wearing his black overcoat and white turban? He now sits on a chair in front of his bed, next to the stove, wearing only black trousers and a freshly ironed white shirt. We exchange pleasantries. How is your health, I ask three times. And then, after half an hour, I ask the question that has been on my mind all this time: 'What on earth has happened?' The mufti sighs and smiles: 'Ah, politics is like the weather in March. You can expect anything.' After that it is mainly Omer who speaks. While the mufti's wife brings tea and joins us in the small room, he tells the story of the sudden dismissal, the appointment of interim muftis and the announcement of the election.

The election is a source of resentment to everyone in the room. 'We have always had the system that a group of fourteen theologians and politicians from our Muslim community would nominate a number of candidates to the Greek government and they would select one and appoint that person as mufti.' Omer takes his time to explain the system to me. 'This is also how it works with the Greek community in Turkey. But now the Greek government has appointed new muftis without any consultation, and suddenly they are talking about elections. Nowhere in the world are muftis elected!'

The discussion goes on for half an hour about whether these elections will actually take place or whether they are a political ploy to keep Turkey happy. 'After all, we still have their helicopter pilots!' Mehmet explains to me, referring to the incident where Greek border soldiers were arrested by Turkey, and Greece subsequently arrested the pilots of a Turkish military helicopter that had made an emergency landing in Greece.

Their resentment about the state of affairs does not fade. It is striking how 'the government' is mentioned time and again. This is understandable, but it also gives the impression of self-pity and victimhood. Poor us, whose rights are violated all the time. I try to give the conversation another twist: 'Suppose the Treaty of Lausanne were to be denounced,' I say to Omer, 'and you were appointed Minister, how would you settle the whole issue of the Muslim minority?' He looks perplexed and begins an elaborate explanation of Greece's commitments under the Treaty of Lausanne and other human rights treaties.

'No, no,' I interrupt him. 'I mean this as a thought experiment. Let's assume the situation were a blank page, and it were up to you to fill it in without having to bother about any treaties, or Turkey or the Greek government. What would it look like then? What would be your preferred situation?'

Omer sits still, staring silently at the ceiling for a while and then he bursts into laughter: 'But I can't think like that! I'm completely shaped by our history and circumstances.' And then the conversation returns to the angry litany about the Greek government that misunderstands the rights of the Thracian Muslim minority that were given to them by the treaties of a century ago.

When the mufti's wife enters with coffee, I know that is the signal for the end of the visit. I carefully sip the Turkish coffee and then start with the ritual of saying goodbye. The mufti looks up, startled: 'No, no, what are you doing? If you visit a second time, we have to eat. I invite you to a fish dinner in a village on the coast.' I politely decline the offer and say that I really must go, but he is serious. I now understand that he had put on his fine clothes with the idea of going out. And it comes in handy that I came by car, so I can drive them all to the restaurant. I accept the offer and we go outside. The mufti has to be supported by Omer and gets into the car with great difficulty. His wife is squeezed in between Mehmet and Omer on the backseat; I need to drop her off at her sister's, three blocks down the road.

We drive through the midday heat to a harbour town on the coast, half an hour from the mufti's village. The tavern overlooking the sea has a table reserved for us. Once seated on the terrace, the mufti looks out over the sea and sighs with satisfaction. 'I used to fish here,' he says softly. While Omer and Mehmet place orders to fill the table with fish dishes, the mufti tells us how he went fishing at sea every week with friends at sea. Apparently, his fishing career has been longer than his career as mufti. I now remember that when I first tried to get in touch with the mufti through Ioannis, he had told me several times that the mufti could not be reached because he was out fishing. At the time I thought Ioannis was making this up to keep me at bay.

After a sumptuous meal, I drive everyone home. It is quiet in the car. When we say goodbye, the mufti says cheerfully: 'Goodbye. Here, or in the hereafter.' It is the last time I would see him. He would pass away half a year later, in December 2019.

When I first came to Western Thrace more than a year ago, I mainly had questions about the functioning of Islamic family law and the sharia court. But now the question has broadened: the sharia court and Islamic family law in Thrace are intimately linked to the Muslim community, and before we delve into the legal intricacies, we must first consider the position of this minority. After all, what is a Muslim minority? And what rights do they want, what rights have they been granted and what rights should they have? Are they allowed to live by rules that are different from those of the rest of the nation? These are much bigger questions than the mechanisms of a sharia court, and they are the questions that the whole of Europe is wrestling with when it comes to religion, in general, and Islam, in particular.

It all seems so deceptively simple. When we speak of a 'Muslim minority', the hallmark of this group is its religion, Islam. Is that not so? But it does not appear to be so straightforward here in Western Thrace. Take for instance the affirmative action that the Greek government has introduced for the benefit of the Muslim minority to make it easier for them to enter the civil service and higher education. The reason for this, I was told, is that their degree of proficiency in the Greek language is below average because they mostly speak Turkish at school and, in the cases of the Pomaki or Roma, also that language at home.

This affirmative action is especially prevalent in higher education, in particular in the study of medicine, where selection is based on examination results. Someone from the Muslim minority with lower grades than a Greek Christian is then still allowed to study. I once suggested that it would be smart for a Greek Christian with low grades to convert to Islam so that he would be allowed in. I meant this as a joke, but the response I got was serious and firm: no, that is not possible. But why not, I insisted. The newly appointed mufti of Komotini gave me a clear answer: because this convert does not belong to the Muslim minority. 'The community is the community. They have been granted that special status by the Treaty of Lausanne. They are who they were then, and who they are now. You cannot become member of that community by conversion.'

The mufti knows what he is talking about. He regularly has to issue statements on behalf of Thracian Muslim youngsters confirming that they belong to the Muslim community. With that they can get dispensation for their lower grades and enter university. Such a declaration cannot be issued lightly: 'Greece applies the European rules that religion may not be a reason for discrimination. This affirmative action is an exception to that rule.' In order to draw up the statement, however, he does not so much check whether the person in question is Muslim. 'No, I do a full background check into the family tree, to see if they are really from our community.'

Being a Muslim who lives in Thrace, therefore, is not the same as being a member of the Thracian 'Muslim minority'. And if one is not a member of the Muslim minority, one cannot claim the rights of that community. That is what happened to a Muslim Syrian and his Greek wife who had converted to Islam. This Muslim couple had settled in Thrace. The Syrian had been a practising physician in Aleppo but needed to get some additional diplomas from Greek medicine school in order to be fully qualified to open his own practice in Greece. However, his Syrian grades and diplomas were not sufficient for admission to Greek medicine school. But when he applied for the special arrangement for Thracian Muslims, he was refused. He might be a Muslim living in Thrace, but he was not a member of the Thracian 'Muslim minority' and therefore not entitled to the special treatment.

It is not possible to become a member of this Muslim community. But neither can one leave that community. This was explained to me by the human rights professor in Thessaloniki. He told me the story of someone from the Thracian Muslim community who was an atheist and had applied for a job as a history teacher at a 'Greek minority' school (formerly called a 'Turkish' school) in Western Thrace. Although his qualifications as a teacher were excellent, he was turned down. It was the same issue I had heard before: certain subjects are taught in Turkish and are therefore assigned to teachers who are Thracian Muslims, while other subjects are taught in Greek, and they can only be taught by Christians. This teacher was from the Thracian Muslim minority but said that he had abandoned his faith and declared himself to be non-Muslim. And since his Greek was fluent, why could he then not teach those courses? But the rule was applied strictly: he came from the Turkish-speaking Muslim community and was therefore not allowed to teach history in Greek. 'This is ridiculous, of course, but I have heard stories like this before,' the professor said. Then he grinned: 'I'm thinking of making this my next court case.'

The Muslim community of Western Thrace is thus like a Muslim tribe: you belong to it by birth, and you cannot leave it, not even if you renounce Islam, just as an outsider who converts to Islam cannot become a member of the tribe. This goes beyond an Ottoman *millet*:

there, you could get in or out by converting (except, of course, when you were a Muslim[4]). The Thracian Muslim community is unique in that it did not grow naturally over the centuries but was created by a treaty. I noticed in my discussions with these Muslims what kind of schizophrenia that has brought about: on the one hand, they claim special community rights that apply only to them; on the other, they want to be treated in accordance with international human rights standards. But a mix of the communal and individual approach seems impossible.

At the same time, this group of Muslims has also grown special – or has been made special, I should say – by circumstances. First of all, they are geographically isolated in an area that is like a dead end, sandwiched between the mountains in the north and the sea in the south, ending at the narrow Turkish border in the east. This has led to social and economic isolation. A similar isolation had befallen them politically, with Greece until recently considering them to be foreigners living in Greece, while Turkey considers them to be Turks living abroad.

And on top of all that, this community has regularly been the victim of situations beyond their control. They were the subject of a treaty that was concluded over their heads. As a result, they became a plaything in the political tensions between Greece and Turkey, which took their mutual grievances and conflicts out on the Greek and Turkish minorities. These conflicts were compounded with yet another conflict that was played out in this region: the Cold War, with Greece acting as a buffer against Balkan communism. All those years, the Muslim communities living in this small stretch of land at the outer tip of Europe were caught between the hammer and the anvil. It is not surprising that this has marked them and made their exceptional position even more special.

---

4 In the Islamic system of the Ottoman Empire, Muslims were not allowed to convert to another religion, but members of other religions were allowed to convert to any other religion.

I had put the question to Omer, the advisor to the mufti, and now I put it to Selin: if you were governor of Western Thrace, how would you organize it? What do you think would be the ideal situation for Muslims?

We meet on a terrace in the city park, with tables and chairs under the canopy of big trees. Selin has become the proud mother of a healthy son. It is nice to see her again. She is so optimistic and positive, so activist and so proud of both her Thracian background and the fact that she is Greek that I think to myself that she should actually become president of Greece. I ask her if she has ever considered going into politics. To my surprise, she nods vigorously: 'A friend asked if I wanted to stand as a candidate in the local elections, and I was very tempted, but I have my hands full with that little boy of mine right now. I guess I will wait a year or two.'

When I ask her about her imaginary governorship of Thrace, she does not hesitate: 'I would abolish sharia family law and only have Greek law. Still, I do want a mufti who can lead and advise the Muslims in their Islam, but he must be elected, every five or ten years. And Turkey must not interfere with us, because we are Greek and must manage our own affairs.

That is a lot more succinct than Omer's answer. He was still too attached to the Treaty of Lausanne. 'But,' Selin adds after some thought, 'the Greek government must see us as Greeks. So no longer as a security risk, or as a chess piece in its political games with Turkey. We must be recognized as a Greek Muslim minority.'

That brings me to another question: what does it actually mean to be a Muslim minority in Greece? Selin shrugs: 'I don't know. We are just Muslim.' And Turkish? 'Yes, Turkish too. And Pomak and Roma.'

When I had put this to the elected mufti Ibrahim Serif during my previous visit, his colleague whom I suspected to be with the consulate had reacted strongly: 'We are all Turkish! Only Turkish! Pomaks and Roma are no different from Turkish families, or tribes if you will, of the Turkish people.' These were almost exactly the same words Erdogan had used during his visit to Western Thrace a year ago. The consulate man had also referred to the Treaty of Lausanne: 'The treaty says that we have freedom of education in our own language, and Turkish is explicitly mentioned.' That was a liberal interpretation of the treaty, which does not mention the Turkish language, but only establishes the right for the 'Muslim minority' to speak in 'any language' and to receive education in 'their own language'.[5] But the treaty is also drafted in such a way that it inevitably leads to this kind of misunderstanding.[6]

So far, I have discussed mainly the issues of the Muslims in Thrace. What about all the other Muslims in Greece: the Muslim 'community' of Kos and Rhodes and all the 'New Muslims' like the Sudanese whom the new mufti had been talking to on the phone – what should their status be? Should there be a national mufti who is the spiritual leader of all Muslims in Greece? I had put the question to Omer, and now I put it to Selin. The question confuses them both: it is already complicated to try to think out of the box about the best possible situation for the Thracian Muslims, but to include *all the* Muslims of Greece in that picture... Omer and Selin are so preoccupied with the problems and circumstances of the Thracian Muslim minority that it is too much to take in more than that.

'But what about your country, the Netherlands? And how about the rest of Europe?' These are questions that I am regularly being asked these days, often with the unspoken expectation that Europe 'out there', this champion of human rights, might have answers to Thracian problems. This question is not easy to answer because every European country has its own distinct way of dealing with religion and religious minorities. Take the notion of separation of church and state, for instance. In countries such as Belgium, Germany, United Kingdom, Austria, Bosnia or North Macedonia there is a system of

---

5   Arts. 39 and 40 of the Treaty of Lausanne.
6   The Treaty of Lausanne does not speak of ethnicity but only of nationality. According to the treaty, the Turkish subjects in Western Thrace lose their Turkish nationality at the time the treaty comes into force (Art. 30). But in the rights that the treaty lays down for this minority, it consistently speaks of 'Turkish nationals' for the simple reason that they had not yet lost that nationality at the time the treaty was drawn up.

state recognition of religions. The reason for this is mainly financial: in Belgium, the clergy of a recognized religion receive a salary from the state (so they are actually civil servants), in Germany recognized religions can start their own university programmes, in Bosnia and North Macedonia every recognized religious community receives money from the government for clergy salaries, religious education and maintenance of places of worship. But from a Dutch or French perspective, such an arrangement between state and religion would be perceived as a violation of freedom of religion and an infringement of the principle of separating church and state: should religious communities not be free from any state involvement, this being recognition, financing, employment or any other kind of influence? From the perspective of the Bosnians and many others, however, this recognition and financing is exactly what freedom of religion demands: does not the state have the duty to make that freedom possible by creating political, financial and other spaces for the religious communities to celebrate their religion?

Another source of differentiation within Europe is the notion of secularism. This is the position that the state takes vis-à-vis religion. France represents one end of the spectrum with the position of *laïcité*. This means that there should be no representations of religion in places with a state function, such as post offices, banks, state schools, parliament. France is the only European country where religious political parties are not allowed, and one will not see a headscarf in parliament. Indeed, the banning of burkas on the streets and headscarves in state-sponsored places are just one example of how rigorous France can be in implementing that principle. On the other end of the spectrum we might position a country like Italy, where Catholicism is considered so much part of the natural fabric of state and society, that the demand by a parent to have crucifixes removed from the walls of a public school was denied on the grounds that these religious symbols were to be considered part of Italian culture. In the middle we find a country like the Netherlands where the state considers itself religiously neutral – meaning that it has no religious or anti-religious preferences – but allows the public to use, shape or express religion according to their own wishes. This includes women with headscarves in public services and in parliament. But not in uniformed services, like the police or the judiciary. In that respect, the United Kingdom is more flexible, having made the headscarf part of the police woman's uniform.

The differences among European countries concerning their dealings with religion are therefore considerable. What they have in common, however, is the individual approach to religion. And that also shapes the way they deal with minorities. One may talk about religious communities such as Jews or Lutherans or Catholics or Orthodox or Muslims, but such categories actually carry little weight. What has political and legal significance for most European countries is not so much who or what these groups *are*, but what their individual members *do* in the name of their religion. These individual actions are the issues at stake in European countries and much less so the rights of religious minorities. Lawsuits about such matters are never about what rights one may have as a Muslim or a Catholic, but about the question of what room the freedom of religion offers to that particular believer. This is difficult to explain to the Thracian Muslims. The question of which religion is involved, or of who or what the minority in question is, is not relevant, I keep telling them. But they look at me in slight bewilderment. No wonder, because that is the difference between the communal and the individual approach.

The Thracian Muslims often ask me about this freedom of religion. How does that work out in Western Europe? This freedom is almost absolute, I tell them, because it cannot easily be obstructed by the state. The issues with headscarves are one of the main exceptions. And there are other limits to this freedom, of course: child marriages are not allowed, and a religious procession taking place in the middle of rush hour will be prohibited. But apart from that, one is practically free to have one's own idea of what religion is and how it should be practised. That is also the reason why so many Muslims in Western Europe embrace and cherish this freedom, because it enables them to organize their religion according to their own wishes.

When I say this, I sense some jealousy on the part of Greek Muslims: they want this too! But then I tell them about the second great freedom that we cherish in Western Europe: the freedom of speech. That is perhaps even more absolute than the freedom of religion, because it allows for severe forms of criticism about religion.

This frightens the Greek Muslims. They find such insolent behaviour unimaginable. Should that not be regulated, should there not be clear boundaries of respect for religion?

Between these two freedoms of religion and opinion lies a field of tension. For example, at the same time that the Molla Sali case was being decided, the Christian-right Nashville declaration had been published in America and was shortly thereafter adopted in my country by a large number of Dutch Protestants, including several members of parliament. In this declaration issues such as homosexuality were condemned in no uncertain terms. Was this group of Christians breaking the law? No, they have the freedom to express their opinions, however much that may offend others. On the other hand, critics – and even the government officials – also made use of that same freedom and gave these Christians a piece of their mind. It was not a pretty sight, the way they were going at each other.

At this point in my story, I see that people like Selin, Mehmet and Omer start to look glassy-eyed. It has become too abstract for them. The human rights professor from Thessaloniki, on the other hand, finds this interesting. This is the stuff that he deals with, that he tries to make sense of. It is about how people relate to each other in a society. All those groups and individuals with their particular views and behaviours that can differ so much from one another, how should they fit together in a single society? Can everyone do what they want, or should there be a yardstick? And if so, who determines that yardstick?

When I put this question to my students, the first reaction is always that everything should be allowed and that we should all be tolerant of each other. That is what the Greek Muslims say too. It is the harmonious picture that Selin and the barista paint of the Thracian society they live in. But the problem is that this view is not necessarily shared by the religious views of the communities that Selin and the barista belong to. According to the family laws of both the Muslims and the Greek Orthodox, people like Selin and the barista would not able to marry each other, for instance. Likewise, the Christians of the Nashville Declaration are using their freedom to express a view on homosexuality that is blatantly discriminatory and offensive. And according to the family laws of Jews and Muslims, the woman has no right of divorce, while Catholics believe that women are unsuitable for the priesthood. So much for the dream of loving coexistence in harmony and equality.

My students always react with a mixture of confusion and indignation: that is discrimination! Surely the Constitution does not allow this? That is certainly the case, but according to that same Constitution we also have freedom of religion, and that gives the right to hold different opinions and to live one's life according to religious convictions that are in contrast to the Constitution. This right includes holding views that are a philosophy of life for one person but can be seriously offensive to another. For example, a couple kissing in the street can be as offensive to one person as the burka is to another. What is more, this freedom to be different is not limited to religion. It is a foundation of European society. The same European Court that ruled in the Molla Sali case had said more than forty years earlier that the freedom to hold and exchange opinions was the cornerstone of a democratic society, even if those opinions might 'shock, offend or disturb' other people.[7]

It becomes more complicated when we realize that a religious person or minority may claim a right that they are not willing to grant to someone else. For example, the orthodox Christian who is refused as a teacher in a public school because of his religious views on creation and sexuality might – rightly so! – sue the school for discrimination. But that same teacher may not find it strange if a Christian school refuses a teaching position to someone who is homosexual. I have experienced similar differences in attitude in discussions on marital relations. People who are indignant about the fact that homosexual male couples cannot formally legalize their relationship with the biological mother of their child are equally indignant about another marital relationship that, according to this same logic, should also be possible, namely Islamic polygamous marriage.

It seems to me that the notion of freedom of religion gives rise to two kinds of discussions in today's Europe: one is about the rights

---

7   ECHR, 7 December 1976 (*Handyside*).

of religious minorities, and the other is about freedom, that is the freedom to be different and to think differently. The first discussion is what the Greek Muslims are preoccupied with. The issue they are struggling with is not about offensive manners or deviant behaviour but about rights and powers. In that legal battle they beat each other and the government over the head with laws, traditions and treaties.

This Greek discussion takes place within the communitarian tradition that is so different from the individual tradition that is embraced in most of Europe. The communitarian tradition has its advantages, because it gives the believers a sense of bonding, security and support and offers opportunities for far-reaching forms of religious and legal self-government. But for someone like myself, who comes from the individualistic tradition, I see mainly its disadvantages. From my long-term research in the Middle East, and now also in Greece, I conclude that people living in the communitarian tradition are preoccupied with determining who does and who does not belong to that community and who is allowed or not allowed to make use of certain rights that arise from membership of that community. To me, that is not what religious rights and freedoms are supposed to be about.

I drive along the broad motorway, back to Thessaloniki. From Komotini it is a drive of almost three hours. The sea is on my left and the mountains on my right. It gives me time to reflect on the impressions of my trips to this region. With all the talk lately of minorities, I have almost forgotten the original reason that brought me to this part of Greece: what is a sharia court doing here? I now add a new question: what would I think if such a court also existed in other European countries? This is not a theoretical question. I have regularly spoken with Dutch Muslims about their wish to be allowed to settle mutual disputes in the area of family law according to Islamic law. For all sorts of reasons, this is regarded as undesirable or even subversive in the Netherlands. In the United Kingdom, where Muslims have taken the next step by creating so-called Islamic councils, they are met with the same criticism and concern. But the urgent need for some kind of tribunal that can preside over disputes in accordance with the rules of Islam remains a strong desire among Muslims. So what to do?

I ask myself the question that I have regularly asked Greek Muslims in the past few days: if I were allowed to organize things myself, what would be the ideal situation for all those religious and non-religious people in European countries? According to our constitutions and treaties and conventions, we hold that everyone should have the right to be different, and that everyone is entitled to live their lives in accordance with their beliefs, but how far does that right go? Are Jews, Catholics and Muslims allowed to have their own legal systems? These are legal systems with which I would disagree personally, but who am I to condemn it when people – adult people, mind you – think that these rules are of great importance to them?

This was the core of the conversation I had at the time with the Arab lawyer: are communities – religious, ethnic, national or otherwise – allowed to live by their own legal system, or must everyone be subject to the same law? It is interesting that such allowances are made for foreign nationals: all European countries allow foreigners to have their own family laws applied. The French court will apply Swedish marriage or divorce law to Swedes living in France, the Spanish court will do the same with German inheritance law to Germans living in Spain. But somehow it is considered entirely different when it is about our own nationals: everyone within a state should be subject to the same national law, regardless of their own ethnic, religious or even national identities.

But on a closer examination, this one-rule-fits-all does not seem to be that strict. Under the umbrella of national law, people are allowed to maintain and apply all sorts of different regulations, and even appoint some sort of 'judges' to adjudicate in conflicts. Student societies, football unions, associations of lawyers or journalists – to name but a few examples – have regulations and tribunals that settle conflicts. Medical professionals have complaints committees that rule according to their own internal guidelines, and many contractors are members of an arbitration institute where the parties may appoint their own arbitrators to settle the conflict according to certain rules. Similarly, Catholics, Protestants and Jews have their tribunals where they settle conflicts within the community in accordance with their own internal rules. So why not something similar for Muslims?

I am still thinking aloud here. The key question is the extent to which such alternative legal systems may deviate from the national legal system. In principle, the answer should be a resounding 'no'. Yet when it comes to religious institutions, the freedom of religion makes it possible to have rules that are contrary to the constitutional idea of equality and non-discrimination. The Catholic Church may uphold the rule that no woman can become priest, Jews may live in accordance with the rule that only the husband can divorce his wife, orthodox Protestants may deny their womenfolk the right to take on any political functions.

Religious tribunals would therefore have a right to exist. But that should not be a licence for these institutions to do as they please. To me, there are at least three lines that cannot be crossed. The first is the limited reach of one's religious views. A religious community can have internal rules that may be offensive or discriminatory to others, but these rules may not be enforced outside its community. If believers want to subject themselves to rules that are incomprehensible or even reprehensible to outsiders, that is up to them, as long as they do not impose them on others or use them to deliberately offend outsiders.

The second line is the penal code. People may in the name of religion submit themselves to the most bizarre rituals and behaviour as long as these do not conflict with criminal law. Female circumcision or honour killing may be interpreted as a religious command among certain communities but is not so according to criminal law. The same is the case for marriage of minors. It has been suggested that such behaviour might be considered a 'cultural exception' to criminal law, but I do not see the need or the justification of such loopholes in the penal code.

The third line that I would draw is that this freedom to live in accordance with one's religion applies only to adults. If parents or grandparents were to perform female circumcision on minors, then that is a criminal offence according to the Penal Code. But if an adult woman wants to undergo it herself, she is free to do so, just like any other body alterations like tattoos, nose jobs and piercings. The same applies to marriage. If adult women want to submit to a Jewish, Protestant, Islamic or other religious law in which their position is clearly less than that of the man, that is their own choice; a stupid choice perhaps, and one that many people – including me – find bizarre, but it is their right to be different and to live according to their own convictions. But if such a marriage is concluded with minors, then this is a criminal offence.

There is much debate about this voluntarism of adults. Is the choice of Muslim, Jewish, Catholic, Protestant and other women to live according to more orthodox forms of their religion completely voluntary? Are they not forced to do so by their upbringing, their environment, by peer pressure? Outsiders often assume this because in their view it is incomprehensible that anyone would voluntarily submit to such a system. Yet, surprisingly often, these women make their own, well-considered choices. Surely, there will certainly be peer pressure within communities, but is that not the case within all types of social groups and communities? To my mind, the bystanders – that is the government and the not-so-religious majority of society – therefore have a choice to make: either they make sure that the entire population is educated with the idea that they have the freedom to choose, or they make that choice themselves and ban certain practices outright.

All these considerations are of a principled legal nature. Let us, for the sake of argument, pursue this thought of a sharia court from other angles. Is there a place for such an institution in any European society? For many European Muslims this is mainly a practical question motivated by religious interests, but for the rest of the Europeans it is mostly a political issue.

The practical dimension is that the Muslim faithful are in need of organizing certain matters like marriage and divorce according to the rules of Islam. And when any conflict arises, they would like to solve it according to those same rules. The political dimension concerns the question of how a given country in Europe wants to organize its society within the framework of freedoms that they hold dear. Roughly speaking, this can work two ways. The 'liberal' approach would be that people are allowed to regulate their own lives, no matter how strange or shocking others may find it. In that political perspective the state should keep as much distance as possible from the way people choose to live. The other approach, which I call the 'social' approach, believes that the weaker members of society must be protected. And that is a task of the state.

Usually, the social dimension dominates the European discussions about sharia courts. The argument mostly heard is that such courts are to be banned in the interest of Muslim women. They are to be protected because they are considered to be in a vulnerable position twice over: they are the victims of the Islamic legal system, which is disadvantageous to women, and most of them belong to a community that is socio-economically fragile and therefore in need of extra protection. These arguments are often completed by the security argument that the existence of sharia courts would cause Muslims to be even more isolated than they already are and so encourage a radical orthodox variant of Islam, which would form an obstacle to the successful integration of Muslims in society. The gist of all the counterarguments is that Muslims should be forbidden to establish something like a 'sharia court' in order to protect them against themselves.

As much as I agree with the arguments against a sharia court, I am more of the 'liberal' view and would argue that adult Muslims should be able to exercise their freedoms as they see fit even if that includes making choices that I strongly disagree with. Of course, there will certainly be peer pressure within communities to make certain choices. But at least this pressure is not from the state, as was the case until recently in Greece, where the state decided who should make use of sharia courts. And, more importantly, neither should there be any pressure from the state *not to* use such institutions. This opinion draws from my experiences with the ways European states deal with Islam, in general, and sharia courts, in particular: my overall observation is that coercion by a government usually backfires, even when it is motivated by the best of intentions.

Evening has fallen in Thessaloniki, but it is still oppressively hot. I had arrived in the early afternoon and defied the heat by visiting the house where Kemal Atatürk, the founder of the modern Republic of Turkey who signed the Treaty of Lausanne, was born. It was a surprise to me that he came from this city. But I was told that many of the 'Young Turks', which was the movement that wanted to replace the Islamic Ottoman Empire with a secular republic, were not from Turkey but from this region. Now, a century later, the situation seems to be reversed: republican and secular Turks who are fleeing Erdogan's Islamist policies are settling in Greece in large numbers. One of the motivations is undoubtedly the possibility for Turks to buy Greek property, which was one of the many measures the Greek government had recently taken to overcome its stifling economic crisis.

After my wanderings through the midday heat, I took a shower and put on some fresh clothes, and I am now sitting on the terrace of a small café. Around me, the nightlife has started, and young people stroll the streets in their best and shortest outfits. I order a beer and open my notebook to write down the thoughts that came to mind during today's drive. While doing so, I suddenly remember that years ago, shortly after my first visit to Thessaloniki with the students in 2008, I had organized a meeting at my university with a number of prominent Dutch Muslims to discuss the possibilities and impossibilities of a sharia court in the Netherlands. We started off by agreeing that the main obstacle to a free discussion about such a conflict resolution institution was its name. 'Anything that has "sharia" in its name is bound to raise hysterical discussions,' someone said. 'It is as if we want to establish Taliban rule here.' We started that meeting by agreeing to avoid the S-word and focus on the content.

What struck me in that round-table discussion, and in the many conversations I had with Muslims afterwards, was the practical nature of their ideas. 'Dutch society is so focused on the issue of divorce,' one of the participants said, 'but for us, Muslims, there is much more to marriage. There is the complicated process of partner choice which includes the issues with the families involved, and once married there is the issue of family life itself and everything that comes along with it and where marriage counselling is often needed.'

This 'Islamic institution for conflict resolution' should therefore cover a wider range of marital issues than only divorce. 'Divorce is when it ends. Conflicts arise way before that.' This brought us to the next distinctive quality of this institution. In order to solve or even prevent those conflicts, the solutions should be in accordance with both Islamic *and* national law. I had been approached regularly by Muslims with such a request. For an Islamic marriage, this is not so difficult, because it is not unlike a civil marriage, to be concluded between bride and groom in the presence of two witnesses, except that an Islamic marriage needs Muslim witnesses.

Islamic divorce can also be reconciled with civil law, although that is a bit more tricky. The 'repudiation', that is the unilateral Islamic divorce, is not unlike a civil law divorce because they are both a separation for which in most European divorce laws no reasons need to be given. The main difference, of course, is that in civil law both the husband and the wife are entitled to this right of unilateral divorce, while in Islamic law it is the exclusive right of the husband. That can be remedied, however, with the Islamic rule that a husband can transfer his right of divorce to his wife, so that she also has the same right to divorce as he does. If that is done, then the Islamic divorce is identical to a civil divorce.

Similar solutions can be found for other issues so that Islamic family law can be shaped in such a way that it can fit into the civil legal system, without having to lose its typically Islamic character. But in some cases, the differences cannot be bridged. Islamic inheritance law, for instance, has a system of fixed portions of different sizes allotted to the various heirs, and this cannot be squared with the civil law requirement of equal division of the estate. The only solution to that problem that I have seen so far is that the heirs have agreed beforehand to receive their Islamic shares and then redistribute them among themselves in such a manner that everyone is left with an equal share.

According to the Muslims who attended this round-table session, the ideal situation would not be a 'sharia court' or an 'Islamic centre of conflict resolution', but an 'Islamic family institute' offering guidance in diverse areas related to family life. This institute would be staffed with Muslim scholars knowledgeable about Islamic family law, psychotherapists and relation counsellors, lawyers who know both Dutch and Islamic law, and notaries public who can draw up deeds and agreements that cater to both Islamic and civil law. There will be no need for judges, because only the civil judge can make binding decisions. A Muslim who wants to know the Islamic position on a certain topic can be presented with an advice or ruling issued by one of the scholars of the institute. Whether this Muslims deems that ruling as binding is up to him or her. But it is not a ruling with the same status as the one issued by a judge in a civil court.

The more I think about it, the more it appeals to me. In fact, it seems to me that a similar institution would also meet the needs of many people besides Muslims.

When I check out of the hotel in Thessaloniki the next morning to take a taxi to the airport, and hand the key to the receptionist, he answers with 'Barakaloh' ('You're welcome'). It is a typical Greek expression that I find fascinating because it derives directly from the Islamic phrase: *barak-allah* – 'God's blessing (to you)'. When I told the Christian Greeks this, they were shocked: 'No way!' At the same time, their young people flaunt tattoos in Arabic script. When I told the old mufti, he burst out laughing: 'Really? I never knew that!' Selin was equally surprised: 'But if it is true, then it is the most beautiful symbol of our common society!'

FURTHER READING IN ACADEMIC LITERATURE

Europe

Islam in Europe
The growing corpus of literature on Islam in Europe shows its controversial nature: one may find alarming warnings as well as calm and considerate descriptions. Two eminent contemporary scholars of Islamic history, the American professors Bernard Lewis and Richard Bulliet, represent this dichotomy: Bulliet in his *The Case for a Islamo-Christian Civilization*, (Columbia University Press, 2006) stresses the similarities in the developments and experiences of the two civilizations, while Lewis in *Europe and Islam* (Washington: The AEI Press, 2007) emphasizes their differences. I tried to give a balanced view in my own *A Brief History of Islam in Europe. Thirteen Centuries of Creed, Conflict and Coexistence* (Leiden University Press, 2014), in which the many literature references can help the reader further. And finally, a constant in academic literature is provided by the *Journal of Muslims in Europe* (Brill).

Greece

Muslims in Contemporary Greece
The most comprehensive study on Islam and Muslims in Greece is that by Konstantinos K. Tsitselikis, *Old and New Islam in Greece. From Historical Minorities to Immigrant Newcomers* (Leiden/Boston: Martinus Nijhoff Publishers, 2012). For those who prefer a shorter introduction to the subject, Angeliki Ziaka's article offers a good start: 'Greece. Debates and Challenges' (in: M.S. Berger (ed.), *Applying Sharia in the West. Facts, Fears and the Future of Rules of Islam on Family Relations in the West*, Leiden University Press, 2013, pp. 125-138). A good complement to that article is Iris Boussiakou, 'Religious Freedom and Minority Rights in Greece: the case of the Muslim minority in western Thrace' (GreeSE

Paper No. 21, *Hellenic Observatory Papers on Greece and Southeast Europe*, December 2008).

The Population Exchange Between Greece and Turkey
A thorough study of the subject is the book by Onur Yıldırım, *Diplomacy and Displacement: Reconsidering the Turco-Greek Exchange of Populations, 1922-1934* (New York: Routledge, 2006). Many monographs have been published on the various Balkan peoples who suffered from ethnic and religious cleansing in the late 19th and early 20th centuries, but for the specific case of Ottoman Muslims I refer to Justin McCarthy's *Death and Exile. The Ethnic Cleansing of Ottoman Muslims, 1821-1922* (Princeton: The Darwin Press, 2012).

Muslims, Christians and Jews in the Balkan Provinces of the Ottoman Empire
The most thorough study of the late Ottoman Empire is Donald Quataert's amazingly brief and comprehensive *The Ottoman Empire 1700-1922* (Cambridge University Press, 2005). The perspective from the Ottoman subjects in the Balkans can be found in Barbara Jelavich, *History of the Balkans, 18th and 19th centuries* (Cambridge University Press, 1983). For a more detailed analysis of the Balkan population see Kemal Karpat, *Ottoman population, 1830-1914: demographic and social characteristics* (University of Wisconsin Press, 1985). A wonderful monograph of the city of Saloniki and its inhabitants is that by Mark Mazower, *Saloniki, City of Ghosts. Christians, Muslims and Jews, 1430-1950* (New York: Alfred Knopf, 2005).

The Issue of Greeks and Italians in Alexandria
I once stumbled upon the judicial pronouncements of this particular situation and then elaborated on it in 'Regulating tolerance: protecting Egypt's minorities' (in: B. Dupret (ed.), *Standing Trial*, London:
I. B. Tauris, 2004, pp. 345-372).

Islamic Law

Sharia
Readable introductions to the subject are the handy *A History of Islamic Law* by Noel J. Coulson (Edinburgh University Press, 1994, new edition) and the more elaborate book by Knut S. Vikør, *Between God and the Sultan: A History of Islamic Law* (Hurst Publishers, 2005). A general overview of all aspects of the Sharia early and modern, theological and political, is offered in *The Ashgate Companion to Islamic Law* (edited by Rudolph Peters and Peri Bearman, Routledge, 2014). For a deeper study of the complex legal mechanisms and theories of sharia, I refer to one of the most eminent researchers in the field, Wael B. Hallaq, *Sharia: Theory, Practice, Transformations* (Cambridge University Press, 2009).

The Role of Muftis
A good introduction is the first chapter of the standard work *Islamic Legal Interpretation. Muftis and their Fatwas*, written by the editors of that book, Muhammad Khalid Masud, Brinckely Messick and David S. Powers (Harvard University Press, 1996). The other chapters in that book also offer interesting insights into the subject. For a more coherent and very good study I refer to *The Ulama in Contemporary Islam: Custodians of Change* by Muhammad Q. Zaman (Princeton University Press, 2002). Another recommendation is the monograph on one of the best-known muftis today: *Global mufti: the phenomenon of Yusuf al-Qaradawi* by Bettina Gräf and Jakob Skovgaard-Petersen (Columbia University Press, 2009).

Islamic Feminism
This is a new area in Islamic thought that has been emerging strongly since the 1980s. Amina Wadud, herself one of the leading women in this field, wrote the important but not so accessible *Qur'an and woman: rereading the sacred text from a woman's perspective* (Oxford University Press, 1999). A more academic overview is offered by Margot Badran in *Feminism in Islam: secular and religious convergences* (London: One World Publications, 2009). The Muslim women's organization Musawah offers an interesting insight into the practical application of feminist theories to Islamic family law with its report *CEDAW and Muslim*

Family Laws: In Search of Common Ground (2012, available online at www.musawah.org/sites/default/files/CEDAWMFLReport2012Edition_1.pdf).

Islamic Family Law
A good introduction to Islamic family law is D. Pearl & W. Menski, *Muslim Family Law* (London: Sweet & Maxwell, 1988). For the particular story of bridal gift in the United Arab Emirates, I have used Jane Bristol-Rhys, 'Weddings, Marriage and Money in the United Arab Emirates' (*Anthropology of the Middle East*, Vol. 2, No. 1, 2007, pp. 20-36). For those who wish to study Islamic inheritance law, which is extremely complex (you have been warned!), I refer to the handbook on this subject by N.J. Coulson, *Succession in the Muslim Family* (Cambridge University Press, 1971).

Inter-Religious (or Interpersonal) Law in the Middle East

Introductions to inter-Religious Law
The system of inter-religious law underlies the discussion on sharia in Greece. However, this system does not apply anywhere in Europe, and this may explain why we have to go back several decades to find literature on this subject. A good introduction is the only article in English on this subject by G. W. Bartholomew, 'Private Interpersonal Law' (*International & Comparative Law Quarterly*, Vol. 1, 1952, pp. 325-344). The standard work, however, is in German, by Klaus Wähler, *Internationales Privatrecht und Interreligiöses Kollisionsrecht* (Bielefeld: IPRax, 1981). Most literature on this subject is written in French, with a good and very readable) introduction by Raoul Benattar, 'Problème de droit international privé dans les pays de droit personnel' (*Recueil des Cours de l'Academie de Droit International de La Haye*, 1967, pp. 1-111).

Application of Inter-Religious Family Law in Some Middle Eastern Countries
The application of inter-religious law varies from country to country, so that those who really want to immerse themselves in it will be forced to read country studies. Syria, Egypt and Israel are illustrative of different applications of interfaith law, and literature suggestions for those three countries are as follows:

Syria: M.S. Berger, 'The Legal System of Family Law in Syria' (*Bulletin d études orientales*, 1997, pp. 49-78). See also Esther van Eijk, *Family Law in Syria* (I.B. Tauris, 2016).

Egypt: M.S. Berger, 'Public Policy and Islamic Law: The Modern Dhimmi in Contemporary Egyptian Family Law' (*Islamic Law & Society*, Vol. 8, No. 1, 2001, pp. 88-136).

Israel: I. Shahar, *Legal pluralism in the Holy City: competing courts, forum shopping, and institutional dynamics in Jerusalem* (Farnham, Surrey: Ashgate, 2015).

Sharia in Europe

Sharia in Europe
The study of sharia in Europe focuses mainly on the situation of private international law, i.e. the rules followed by national courts when applying foreign law, which in some cases may involve Islamic legal rules. There is a lot of literature available on this subject, with good introductions by Andrea Büchler, *Islamic Law in Europe? Legal Pluralism and its Limits in European Family Laws* (Farnham, Burlington: Ashgate, 2011) and Pauline M. Kruiniger, *Islamic Divorces in Europe. Bridging the gap between European and Islamic legal orders* (The Hague: Eleven International Publishing, 2014).

Much less research, however, has yet been done on the everyday practice of sharia by European Muslims in their own communities, i.e. outside the national courts (with the exception perhaps of England, see below). I have described an overview of these practices and the European legal and political responses to them in my 'Understanding Sharia in the West' (*Journal of Law, Religion and State*, Vol. 1, No. 1, 2018, pp. 236-273). An argument for how sharia can be incorporated into European legal systems can be found in Dominic McGoldrick, 'Accommodating Muslims in Europe: From Adopting Sharia Law to Religiously Based Opt Outs from Generally Applicable Laws' (*Human Rights Law Review*, Vol. 9, 2009, pp. 603-645).

Sharia Courts and Islamic Law in Greece
The most solid and insightful article on this topic is by Yüksel Sezgin, 'Muslim Family Laws in Israel and Greece: Can Non-Muslim Courts Bring about Legal Change in Shari'a?' (*Islamic Law & Society*, Vol. 24, 2017, pp. 1-38). İlkerTsavousoglou's article provides the women's perspective: 'The Legal Treatment of Muslim Minority Women under the Rule of Islamic Law in Greek Thrace' (*Oslo Law Review*, Vol. 3, 2015 (Special Issue: Legal Pluralism), pp. 241-262). Konstantinos Tsitselikis, the lawyer who brought the case of Molla Sali to the European Court of Human Rights, compiles his knowledge and views in 'Muslims of Greece: a Legal Paradox and a Political Failure' (in: Norbert Oberauer, Yvonne Prief and Ulrike Qubaja (eds.), *Legal Pluralism in Muslim Contexts*, Leiden: Brill, 2019). For a discussion of the Molla Sali case itself, I refer to my article 'The Last Shari'a Court in Europe: On *Molla Sali v. Greece* (ECHR 2018)' (*Journal of Islamic Law*, Vol. 1, No. 1, Spring 2020, pp. 115-134).

Sharia 'Courts' and Islamic Law in the United Kingdom
The United Kingdom is unique in Europe for its large number of *sharia councils*, and there is a lot of literature on the subject. A good introduction is the report *The independent review into the application of sharia law in England and Wales Presented to Parliament by the Secretary of State for the Home Department by Command of Her Majesty*, February 2018 (available online at various sites). High-profile lectures by leading figures who have greatly influenced the debate include those by the Archbishop of Canterbury, Dr Rowan Williams, 'Civil and Religious Law in England' (lecture of 7 February 2008, available online on various sites), and by Lord Phillips, Lord Chief Justice, 'Equality Before The Law' (lecture of 3 July 2008, available online on various sites). For detailed studies I refer to S. Bano, *Muslim Women and Shari'ah Councils, Transcending the Boundaries of Community and Law* (London: Palgrave MacMillan, 2012) and J. Brechin, 'A Study of the Use of Sharia Law in Religious Arbitration in the United Kingdom and the Concerns that this Raises for Human Rights' (*Ecclesiastical Law Journal*, Vol. 15, 2013, pp. 293-315).

Religious Minorities

General
One will not find much about 'religious minorities' in the academic literature, since that subject is discussed mainly in terms of 'freedom of religion'. In contrast, individual religious minorities are frequently discussed on a country-by-country basis: there are plenty of country studies on this subject.

In Greece: Treaty of Lausanne
An introduction to the history of the treaty is provided by Renée Hirshon, 'History's Long Shadow: the Lausanne Treaty and Contemporary Greco-Turkish Relations' (in: O. Anastasakis, Kalypso Nicolaidis en Kerem Oktem (eds. , *The Long Shadow of Europe: Greeks and Turks in the Era of Post-nationalism* (Leiden/Boston: Martinus Nijhoff, 2009, pp. 73-94). Legal aspects of this treaty are discussed by B. Oran, 'The minority concept and rights in Turkey: The Lausanne Peace Treaty and current issues' (in Zehra F. Kabasakal Arat (ed.), *Human Rights in Turkey*, University of Pennsylvania Press, 2007, pp. 35-56).

In Europe: Framework Convention for the Protection of National Minorities
The literature on minorities in Europe deals mainly with Muslims. One of the few studies that discuss the constitutional position of minorities in general in their legal-historical context is the German-language book *Minority Protection in Europe* by Rainer Hofman (Max Planck Institute, 2009, available online). For a comprehensive and very accessible explanation of the European Council's Framework Convention for the Protection of National Minorities, I refer to *The Framework Convention: an essential instrument for managing diversity through minority rights* by the Advisory Committee for the Framework Convention for the Protection of National Minorities (Strasbourg 27 May 2016, available online).

In Islam: Dhimmis and Millet
For this subject I refer to the literature mentioned previously under the heading 'Muslims, Christians and Jews in the Balkan Provinces of the Ottoman Empire'. For a more legal approach to this subject, see

Antoine Fattal, *Le statut légal des non-musulmans en pays d'islam* (Beirut: Imprimerie Catholique, 1958). A thorough study is that of A.M. Emon, *Religious Pluralism and Islamic Law. Dhimmis and Others in the Empire of Law* (Oxford University Press, 2014).

Religion and Religious Law in Europe

Religious Law and Religious Courts in Europe
There is very little academic literature about religious law and courts in Europe. Some of it is discussed in Norman Doe, *Law and Religion in Europe: A Comparative Introduction* (Oxford University Press, 2011) and in 'Framing Multicultural Challenges in Freedom of Religion Terms: Limitations of Minimal Human Rights for Managing Religious Diversity in Europe' by Katayoun Alidadi and Marie-Claire Foblets (*Netherlands Quarterly of Human Rights*, Vol. 30, No. 4, 2012, pp. 460-488). A study about the United States but also relevant to the European context is 'Religious Courts in Secular Jurisdictions: How Jewish and Islamic Courts Adapt to Societal and Legal Norms' by Rabea Benhalim (*Brooklyn Law Review*, Vol. 84, No. 3, Spring 2019, pp. 745-800). More detailed studies on the application and institutionalization of Catholic, Jewish or any of the Protestant laws in Europe are rare and limited to the study of local situations, mostly in premodern times. Islamic law is the only exception (see previously under 'sharia in Europe').

The 'Marital Imprisonment' in Islamic and Jewish Law
This particular situation where secular and religious divorce law interlock so that the woman is 'caged' in her religious marriage is discussed mostly from the perspective of Jewish law (where the 'caged woman' is called *agunah*). A general discussion, albeit in a Canadian setting, is 'Halacha, The "Jewish State" and The Canadian *Agunah*: Comparative Law at the Intersection of Religious and Secular Orders' by Pascale Fournier (*The Journal of Legal Pluralism and Unofficial Law*, Vol. 44, 2012, pp. 165-204). For the French situation see Zvi Jonathan Kaplan's book chapter 'The Plight of the Agunah: The Proposal of the Union des Rabbins Français' (in Simcha Fishbane and Eric Levine (eds.), *Dynamics of Continuity and Change in Jewish Religious Life*, Academic Studies Press, 2018, pp. 226-240). A general analysis

of the similar plight of Muslim women can be found in Zahra Ayubi, 'Negotiating Justice: American Muslim Women Navigating Islamic Divorce and Civil Law' (*Journal for Islamic Studies*, Vol. 30, No. 1, 25 February 2011, pp. 78-102).

The Relationship Between State and Religion
This is a complicated subject, because there is much confusion about terminology such as 'secularism' and 'separation of church and state'. Moreover, a 'European' approach is hardly possible as each European country has its own particular legal, political and social framework to deal with its relationship between state and religion. John Madeley and Frank Cass have made a relatively successful attempt to provide 'A framework for the comparative analysis of church-state relations in Europe' (*West European Politics*, Vol. 26, No. 1, January 2003, pp. 23-25). Most authors suffice with a comparative overview of the various church-state relations, like Gert Pickel and Olaf Müller (eds.), *Church and Religion in Contemporary Europe Results from Empirical and Comparative Research* (Wiesbaden: VS Verlag für Sozialwissenschaften, 2009, whereby I refer to the chapter by Detlef Pollack and Gert Pickel titled 'Church-State Relations and the Vitality of Religion in European Comparison', pp. 145-166). One of the specialists in the field, Silvio Ferrari, also deserves mention, and one of his many lucid analyses on the subject is 'Law and Religion in a Secular World: A European Perspective' (*Ecclesiastical Law Journal*, Vol. 14, No. 3, 2012, pp. 355-370). Although the relation between state and religion (or its institutionalized form) is usually discussed in legal terms, we must not forget that its undercurrents are mostly of a social nature. For this one will find a good introduction in Grace Davie's, 'Religion in Europe in the 21st Century: The Factors to Take into Account' (*European Journal of Sociology*, Vol. 47, No. 2, 2006, pp. 271-296).

The Two Freedoms of Religion and Speech
The criticism of religion, in general, and Islam, in particular, has been called blasphemous and slanderous by some and has been vehemently defended as freedom of opinion by others. A good introduction to the interaction of these two freedoms is *The right to freedom of religion or belief and its intersection with other rights* by Alice Donald and Erica

Howard (Discussion Paper, ILGA-Europe, Middlesex University Research Repository, 2015). How these intricacies play out in the courtroom has been nicely outlined by Malcolm D. Evans in 'From Cartoons to Crucifixes: Current Controversies Concerning the Freedom of Religion and the Freedom of Expression before the European Court of Human Rights' (*Journal of Law and Religion*, Vol. 26, No. 1, 2010-2011, pp. 345-370). For a more detailed discussion of the freedom of religion in the European context, I refer to 'Misperceptions of Freedom of Religion or Belief' by Heiner Bielefeldt (*Human Rights Quarterly*, Vol. 35, No. 1, February 2013, pp. 33-68) and *Religious Liberty and International Law in Europe* by Malcolm D. Evans (Cambridge University Press, 2008).

ABOUT THE AUTHOR

Professor Maurits Berger holds the Sultan of Oman Chair as professor of Islam and the West at Leiden University. His specializations are Islamic law (sharia), Islam in Europe and political Islam.

Berger graduated in Law and in Arabic Studies and wrote his dissertation about Islamic law. He worked as a lawyer in Amsterdam for three years and lived Syria and Egypt for seven years, where he worked as a journalist and researcher in the field of Islamic law. He is a senior research associate at the Clingendael Institute for International Relations and was a member of the Advisory Council on International Affairs of the Dutch Ministry of Foreign Affairs from 2012 to 2019.

As founder and editor-in-chief of the Dutch-language *Journal for Religion, Law and Policy (Tijdschrift voor Religie, Recht en Beleid)*, he believes that topics related to law and religion deserve a platform in both academic and policy circles.

Berger regularly gives courses to imams, diplomats, police and military personnel and acts as an advisor to the government and as an expert for lawyers and the media.